Easy Do It Yourself Computer
Speed-Up & Care Guide!

****

Over 49 Easy, Do It Yourself Tweaks – Tips & Tactics for Optimum Computer Performance and Internet Security

XP Service Pk 3 (SP3), Vista, Windows 7 and Windows 8

EASY FIXES THAT ALMOST ANYONE CAN DO!

A Collection of All the Tools You Need In One Handy Guide! No More Having to Search Online for Answers When Your Computer Crashes, Becomes Infected, Slows to a Crawl, or Just Plain Stops Working Altogether

Aaron 'Cybercoach' Robinson

Most computer problems are relatively easy to fix, and you can save money and time by diagnosing and fixing the problem yourself.

"This Guide Contains Easy, Simple, Step-By-Step Instructions Most Anybody Can Do! Now You Can Increase Your Computer's Speed, Protect Your PC from Infections, and Browse the Internet Safely!"

Easy Do It Yourself Computer Speed-Up & Care Guide!

First Printing, 2013
Copyright© 2013 Lulu Author. Aaron 'Cybercoach' Robinson
All rights reserved.
ISBN 978-1-300-83141-9

All Rights Reserved

Disclaimer: Although the author and publisher have made every effort to ensure that the information in this book was correct at press time, the author and publisher do not assume and hereby disclaim any liability to any party for any loss, damage, or disruption caused by errors or omissions, whether such errors or omissions result from negligence, accident, or any other cause. **NOTE**: I **Do Not** recommend tinkering with the **registry files**. Such activities can be detrimental to your computer and should only be attempted by properly trained professionals.

The information in this book is from tips, tricks and tactics that I use to keep my own computers running at peak performance. Therefore, your use of these methods is at your own risk.

Table of Contents

Table of Contents Con't.

The Quick Check List:
If your Computer is not functioning properly check the items on this list first:
1. Ensure the PC is plugged in to a power supply source and turned on (make sure all components are on: the monitor, the printer)
2. Look for any loose or damaged cables and cords that attach to your computer.
3. Make sure that all of your floppy drives are empty (normally all floppy drives should be empty when booting the computer, unless you want to boot the computer from a floppy disk)
4. If on a network, check with other users of the network in your vicinity to see if their PC's or Mac's are functioning normally. Often a downed network can cause a variety of errors when running applications. The problem may not be with your machine, but with the network.
5. If all of the above seems to be fine, try turning off the computer completely and restart it (cold booting). Sometimes this is enough to reset the software and network connections and get the machine back to working order.

Important Note:
1. Prior to opening your computer's case, check to see if the machine's warranty is still valid. If so return it to the manufacturer for repair, because your messing around inside the case can void the warranty.
2. Also, it is not wise to open up the computer unless you know what you are doing.
3. There is a risk of electrical shock,
4. There is a high risk of damaging the electronic components inside the PC.

PC Checklist Con't.

NOTE: Make a backup copy of any important documents.
First off, you should keep duplicate copies of files that are important to you and would be a loss to you personally if your hard disk fails. Your most important files can easily fit on a USB *flash drive*, or if you prefer, there are several online sites you can choose from, that will back up your data for you. I guarantee that if you make 2 or more backups of the same thing, the chance of a total loss of that data is negligible, and especially so if you store those flash drives / CD or other media in different places. If you do so, you won't be freaked out by virus scares, and crashes. You will rest contently knowing that your important documents and files will not be lost.

Ok, Let's Get Started!

Preface

The personal computer is a great tool if you know how to use it properly, and keep it running at its peak. Likewise, finding ways to **speed up your computer** is the most important thing you could do as a computer user. When you have a slow computer and you are trying to do work on it, you can easily get frustrated to the point of doing something drastic!

In this guide I have compiled tips, tweaks, tactics and recommended software that I am currently using to keep computers running at their best. I show you step-by-step how to use the tools available in **XP Ser-vice Pack 3 (SP3), Vista, Windows 7** and **Windows 8** to more efficient-ly maintain your computer, and safeguard your privacy when you're online, in easy to understand terms. By following a few simple guidelines, you can fix your problem now, maintain your computer and keep it run-ning smoothly with little or no money. Windows PCs typically slow down as applications are installed and used. For example; whether you are using word processing, spreadsheets, internet, games or anything else, hard drives fill with temporary files that do not always get removed when no longer needed, and can slow your computer down. You will also learn how to safely browse the internet, and how to protect your computer from unwanted malware and infections. The **Tips, Tweets** and **Tactics** listed in this guide will help keep your PC running at optimum performance!

Windows 8 Tips, Tricks and Shortcuts

Windows 8 has been out for quite some time now, and if you are used to previous versions of Windows O.S; then you're going to notice the drastically different user interface this new version of Windows ushered in. In fact, Windows 8 has seen the biggest change since the jump from Windows 3.1 to Windows 95. Even experienced PC users may be left feeling a little lost... *Just figuring out something as simple as shutting down your PC can be challenging with Windows 8.*

Preface Con't.

In part, that's because Windows 8 is **two** Operating Systems in one. There's the traditional Windows desktop, which is basically Windows 7 (*it runs the 4 million existing Windows programs*), then there's a new environment designed for tablets and laptops that sport touch-enabled displays. Out goes the Start menu, in comes the new touch-oriented Start screen with new Windows 8-style apps and new interface conventions. Most new PCs will come with Windows 8, and if Microsoft is correct about the world moving to touch screen PCs, sooner or later you'll find a Windows 8 machine under your fingertips. Don't despair though, help is at hand.

I have researched every part of Windows 8, uncovering many of its most important tips, tricks and shortcuts and have listed them in this guide so you can navigate, be more productive and learn your way around Windows 8 as quickly as possible. You will soon be equipped to get the most out of Microsoft's latest release, have some fun and make the new Windows 8 OS a worthwhile choice. With these tips, tricks and shortcuts **(Chapter 5, page 185),** you won't need to spend hours or weeks poking around online for help!

.

A well maintained PC will operate much faster when accessing the internet!

Chapter 1

The Need for Speed!
Easy / Basic Computer Speed-Up Tweaks & Tips

In Microsoft Windows, caches are present to speed up the retrieval of data. Your browser's history, your application data, your file explorer activities, your previous searches, your network adapter information and more, all are stored in the form of caches to make subsequent calls for this data faster.

While this is generally very helpful, caches continue to build up over time, and if they're not addressed every now and then, soon these caches will start bogging the ma-chine down, resulting in a relatively poor user experience over all. Hence, it's quite favorable to clean out your operating system's caches from time to time. In **Windows 8**, this is even more important, since you have both the Desktop/Legacy and Modern environ-ments running side by side, each with its own set of caches.

Disk Cleanup Tool

When my computer is running slower than before, the first thing I do is run the computer's **'Disk Cleanup Tool'.** The *Disk Cleanup tool* helps you free up space on your hard disk to improve the performance of your computer. The tool identifies files that you can safely delete, and then enables you to choose whether you want to delete some or all of the identified files.

Use Disk Cleanup to:

1. Remove temporary Internet files.
2. Remove downloaded program files (such as Microsoft
3. ActiveX controls and Java applets).
4. Empty the Recycle Bin.
5. Remove Windows temporary files such as error reports.
6. Remove optional Windows components that you don't use.
7. Remove installed programs that you no longer use.
8. Remove unused restore points and shadow copies from System Re-store.

Tip: *Typically, temporary Internet files take the most amount of space because the browser caches each page you visit for faster access later. It is important to never permit the free space on your C: drive to be less than 10% of the total size or twice the installed RAM.*

Steps to use Disk Cleanup Tool - Here's How to Do It:
Window 8
To launch the *Disk Cleanup Utility* in Windows 8, right-click the partition of your choice under **Computer,** and select **Properties.** From the dialog box, click **Disk Cleanup** and wait for the tool to load.
Within the **Cleanup utility,** make sure you select everything for maximum effect. At a bare minimum, you need to clean out **thumbnails** and **temporary files**.
Next, click OK to implement the changes.
Windows 7 users follow these steps:
1. Click **Start**, click **All Programs**, click **Accessories**, click **System Tools**.

Note: *You could also type* **cleanmgr** *into the start menu search box and press En-ter to open Disk Cleanup.*

2. Click **Disk Cleanup**. If several drives are available, you might be prompted to specify which drive you want to clean. Typically, this will be 'disk C'.
3. When Disk Cleanup has calculated how much space you can free up, in the **Disk Cleanup for** dialog box, scroll through the content of the **Files to delete** list.
4. Clear the check boxes for files that you don't want to delete, and then click **OK**.

For more options, such as cleaning up System Restore and Shadow copy files, under Description:
1. Click **Clean up system files**, then click the **More Options** tab.
2. When prompted to confirm that you want to delete the specified files, click **Yes**.
After a few minutes, the process completes and the Disk Cleanup dialog box closes, leaving your computer cleaner and performing better.

Free Up Disk Space Con't.

Steps to Use Disk Cleanup Tool - Windows XP users
Here's How to Do It:
1. Click **Start**, point to **All Programs**, point to **Accessories**, point to **Sys-tem Tools**, and then click **Disk Cleanup**. If several drives are available, you might be prompted to specify which drive you want to clean.
2. In the **Disk Cleanup for** dialog box, scroll through the content of the **Files to delete** list.
3. Clear the check boxes for files that you don't want to delete, and then click **OK**.
4. When prompted to confirm that you want to delete the specified files, click **Yes**.
After a few minutes, the process completes and the Disk Cleanup dialog box closes, leaving your computer cleaner and performing better.

Disk Defragmentation

Volume	Session Status	File System	Capacity	Free Space	% Free Space
(C:)	Defragmented	NTFS	27.94 GB	17.81 GB	63 %

Estimated disk usage before defragmentation:

Estimated disk usage after defragmentation:

Analyze   Defragment   Pause   Stop   View Report

■ Fragmented files   ■ Contiguous files   □ Unmovable files   □ Free space

Disk Defragmentation

Disk fragmentation happens to a hard disk over time as you save, change, or delete files. Both the files and the hard disk itself become fragmented over time, and slows down the overall performance of your system. When files are fragmented, the computer must search the hard disk when a file is opened to piece it back together. Therefore, the response time can be significantly longer.

Disk Defragmenter is a Windows utility that consolidates fragmented files and folders on your computer's hard disk so that each occupies a single space on the disk. With your files stored neatly end-to-end, without fragmentation, reading and writing to the disk speeds up.

When to Run Defragmenter In addition to running **Disk Defragmenter** at regular intervals (**monthly is optimal**) other times you should run it is:
1. When you add a large number of files.
2. Your free disk space totals 15 percent or less.
3. You install new programs or a new version of Windows.
NOTE: Windows 8
In Windows 8, the name for a lot of features in Windows 7 has changed. For example: In Windows 8. Disk Defragmenter has now been changed to **Optimize Drives**.

How to use Disk Defragmenter: - Here's How to Do It: Windows 8 Users:

In Windows 8, the drives are automatically scheduled for optimization on a weekly basis. You can manually optimize or defragment a drive in Windows 8 by selecting it and then clicking on the **Optimize** button:

To do this open the **Charms bar** and search for **Optimize Drives.** Or you can still search disk defragmenter and it will load the correct feature. You can also get to the Optimize Drives feature by going to My Computer, selecting a drive, clicking on the **Manage** tab and then clicking on the **Optimize** button.

This will bring up the Optimize Drives dialog box; there you will see a list of your drives and their current status.

Click the Optimize button: This will start the defrag process manually and you'll see that Windows 8 does two passes to relocate fragmented data on the hard drive. You can also click the Analyze button to quickly update the percent fragmented value.

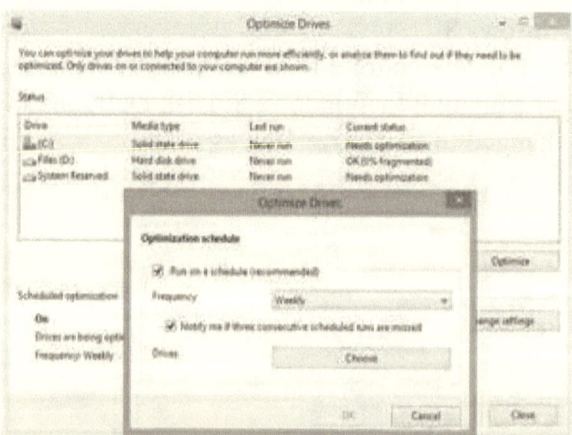

Disk Defragmentation Con't.

If you want to change the automatic optimize schedule, click on
Change settings.
You can either remove the schedule so that automatic
defragmentation is turned off or you can change it from weekly
to daily or monthly. You can also choose all drives or a specific
drive to change the schedule for. Lastly, if you click the Choose
button, you can change whether you want new drives to
automatically be scheduled for optimization also or not.

Windows 7 users:
1. Click Start, click All Programs, click Accessories, click
System Tools, and then click Disk Defragmenter
2. In the Disk Defragmenter dialog box, click the drives that you
want to defragment, and then click the Analyze button. After the
disk is analyzed, a dialog box appears, letting you know whether
you should defragment the analyzed drives.

**Tip: You should analyze a volume before defragmenting it to
get an estimate of how long the defragmentation process will
take.**

3. To defragment the selected drive or drives, click the
Defragment disk button. In the Current status area, under the
Progress column, you can monitor the process as it happens.
After the defragmentation is complete, Disk Defragmenter
displays the results.
4. To display detailed information about the defragmented disk or
partition, click View Report.
5. To close the View Report dialog box, click Close.
Note: Remember your computer might be set up by default to run
Disk Defragmenter automatically. If so, under **Schedule**, it will
read *'Scheduled defragmentation is turned on'*, then displays the
time of day and frequency of defragmentation. You can turn off
automatic defragmentation or change the time or frequency by
following these steps.

Disk Defragmentation Con't.

Here's How to Do It:
1. click the **Configure schedule** (or **Turn on schedule**, if it is not currently configured to run automatically).
2. Next, change the settings, then click OK.
3. To close the Disk Defragmenter utility, click the Close button on the title bar of the window.

How to use Disk Defragmenter - Windows XP
Here's How to Do It:
1. Click Start, point to All Programs, point to Accessories, point to System Tools, and then click Disk Defragmenter
2. In the Disk Defragmenter dialog box, click the drives that you want to defragment, and then click the Analyze button. After the disk is analyzed, a dialog box appears, letting you know whether you should defragment the analyzed drives.

Tip: You should analyze a volume before defragmenting it to get an estimate of how long the defragmentation process will take.

3. To defragment the selected drive or drives, click the Defragment button.

Note: **In Windows Vista, there is no graphical user interface to demonstrate the progress, but your hard drive is still being defragmented.**

After the defragmentation is complete, Disk Defragmenter displays the results.
4. To display detailed information about the defragmented disk or partition, click **View Report**.
5. To close the **View Report** dialog box, click **Close**.
6. To close the Disk Defragmenter utility, click the **Close** button on the title bar of the window.

In addition to running **Disk Cleanup** and **Disk Defragmenter** to optimize the performance of your computer, you can check the integrity of the files stored on your hard disk by running the **Error Checking utility.**

As you use your hard drive, it can develop bad sectors. Bad sectors slow down hard disk performance and sometimes make data writing (such as file saving) difficult, or even impossible. If your computer is running slower than normal it may have errors on the hard drive. You can run the Windows Check Disk utility to diagnose and automatically repair any errors it finds on the drive.
The Error Checking utility is a built-in tool that scans the hard drive for bad sectors, and scans for file system errors to see whether certain files or folders are misplaced.

Note:
In Windows 7 and earlier O.S. versions, checking your hard disk, every once in a while for errors that are usually caused due to improper or sudden shutdowns, corrupted software, metadata corruption, etc, is always a good practice as this can help solve some computer problems and improve the performance of your Windows computer. If you use your computer daily, you should run this utility once a week to help prevent data loss.

Tip: Only select the "Automatically fix file system errors" check box if you think that your disk contains bad sectors.

In **Windows 8**, Microsoft has redesigned **chkdsk utility** - the tool for detecting and fixing disk corruption. In Windows 8, Microsoft introduced a file system called **ReFS**, which does not require an offline **chkdsk** to repair corruptions – as it follows a different model for resiliency and hence does not need to run the traditional **chkdsk** utility.

The disk is periodically checked for file system errors, bad sectors, lost clusters, etc, during Automatic Maintenance.

To manually begin the scan:

1. Right-click on the Drive which you wish to check and select Properties. Next, click on Tools tab and under Error checking, click on the Check button. This option will check the drive for file system errors.

2. If the system detects that there are errors, you will be asked to check the disk. If no errors are found, you will see a message – You don't need to scan this drive. You can, nevertheless, choose to check the drive. Click on Scan drive to do so.

3. The scanning starts. I found that the process ran quite fast and the scanning was over in less than 5 minutes.

4. On completion, Windows 8 will display a message: If no errors are found it will say so.

5. If errors are found, you will see the following message: Restart your computer to repair file system. You can restart right away or schedule the error fixing on next restart.

Windows 7 and earlier O.S. Versions:

Follow these steps to run the Error Checking utility:

1. Close all open files.

2. Click **Start**, and then click **My Computer**.

3. In the My Computer window, right-click the hard disk you want to search for bad sectors, and then click **Properties**.

4. In the **Properties** dialog box, click the **Tools** tab.

5. Click the **Check Now** button.

6. In the **Check Disk** dialog box (called **Error-checking** in Windows 7), select the **Scan for and attempt recovery of bad sectors** check box, and then click **Start**.

If bad sectors are found, choose to fix them.

Pictures, Videos and Large Files can take up an enormous amount of hard disk space. If you want to keep the pictures, videos and music files - and you most likely do - copy them to a CD-rom, or store them on a re-movable USB flash drive to save disk space. Also, large files can either be deleted, or compressed to save space.

Find Large Files Using Windows Search
One way to find files to delete is by using the windows search utility. Windows Search can help you find the largest files on your hard drive.

Here's How to Do This:
1. Click "Start" then click "Search" to open up the windows search dialog window.
2. On the left side of the window, Click "All files and folders", then click the search button.
3. To find the largest files, Order by "Size" descending by clicking on the column heading for "Size" twice.
4. After windows is finished searching, you will have a list of all files on your hard drive ordered from the biggest to smallest. From here you can choose to either completely delete large files from your computer, or you can compress the into smaller 'Zip' files to save space.

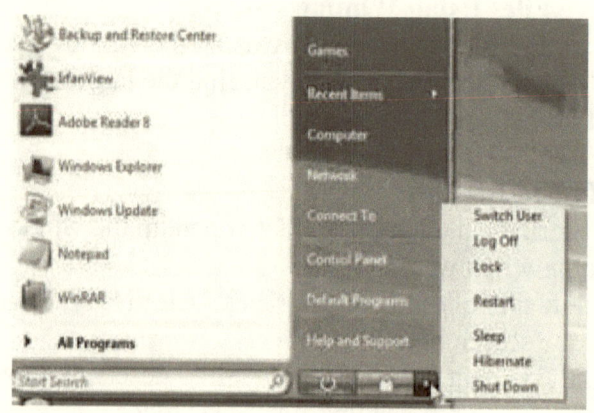

Do a Shutdown/ Reboot:
Insufficient resources such as memory can slow your computer down to a crawl. If your computer is running slow, a *restart* may be the answer by selecting **"Start"**, **"Turn off Computer"** and **"Restart"**. By shutting down your computer and restarting it using the start menu will empty out memory and allow these resources to become available.

Some programs do not release memory properly when they close, and a **warm boot** may become necessary. Sometimes even doing a **warm boot** (restarting the computer without restarting the BIOS also) will not release some of the drivers and other core programs in memory, and may require a **cold boot**.

A **warm boot** is easy to do in both XP and Vista and can save a lot of time by making the boot up process much faster, whereas with a **cold boot** the computer has to be completely shut down and then restarted.

Here's How to Do It - Warm Boot:
To do a **warm boot** all you need to do is hold the *shift key* before you click *'Restart'*. This will invoke a **warm boot** without rebooting the BIOS.

The Windows system is designed to hold on to those programs for a period of time. Shutting down the system for 30 seconds will cause the chips to "forget" the settings, and they will start anew when you restart the sys-tem. Curing these 'Memory Leaks' is as simple as rebooting the machine when it starts getting sluggish.

Do a Shut Down and Reboot Con't

If your computer is frozen and you are unable to do anything, you may have to **cold-boot** your system. A **cold boot** (also called a *hard boot*) is the start-up of a computer from a powered-down, or off, state - For example, when you first turn your computer on after being off for the night, is referred to as cold booting the computer. Some program failures will lock up the computer and require a cold boot to use the computer again.

Here's How to Do It - Cold Boot:
1. Turn the power button off.
2. Wait about 15 seconds or so before turning it back on.
Turning the power off and then back on again clears memory and many internal settings.

Note: Only do a cold boot if it is **absolutely necessary**, because when the machine is cold-booted (i.e. powered off and on again without clean shutdown) you will most likely be operating with a minimal operating system.

Ready Boost

Have you ever had an experience where you are using a lot of programs at the same time in Windows, or a really memory intensive one, and notice that your hard drive activity light is going nuts, there is lots of noise from the hard drive, and your computer is crawling? This is called **disk thrashing** and it is when you have run out of physical RAM and instead Windows is using a file on your hard drive to act as a virtual memory. Since writing and reading to a hard drive is much slower than reading from physical RAM, your computer's performance takes a huge hit.

All about Ready Boost
If you're using **Windows 7, 8** or **Windows Vista,** you can use Ready Boost to speed up your system. A new concept in adding memory to a system, it allows you to use non-volatile flash memory—like a USB flash drive or a memory card—to improve performance without having to add additional memory.

How to Use Ready Boost:
1. Click Start, and then navigate to Computer.
2. Right click the flash drive or memory card icon and choose Properties.
3. Click the Ready Boost tab
4. Select "Use this device" option.
5. Use the "Space to reserve for system speed" slide bar to adjust amount of memory you want to allocate.
The number that originally appears is the maximum amount available to use.
6. Click OK.

Windows Update

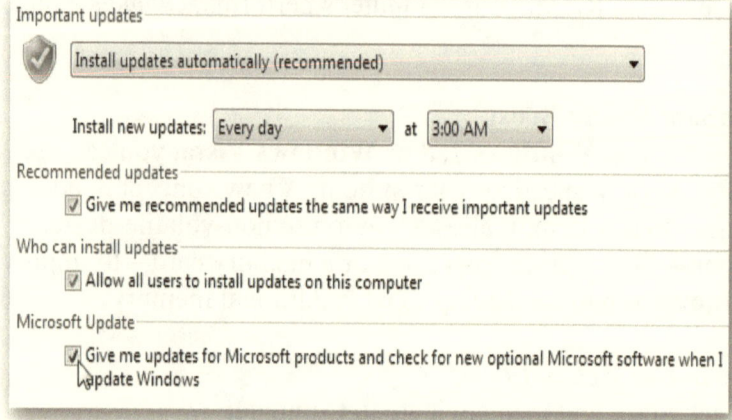

Automate Windows Update

Microsoft releases updates to Windows and other Microsoft products, including Microsoft Office. With Windows Update, you can find and install all these updates, not just the critical ones. Often, the updates can improve your computer's performance.

You can also make your computer a lot safer and stable by automating Windows Update so that your computer downloads and installs all the updates automatically, at a scheduled time, without you having to worry about them.

NOTE: Always click on the **Windows Update icon** that appears in the system tray. Download and install the updates as instructed. You can also visit the Windows Update website to check for updates for your computer.

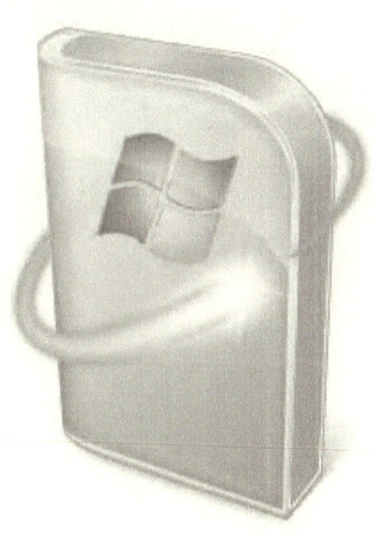

Get the Bugs Out Now!
Time to Find and Remove Those Pesky Bugs!

Find and Remove Infections

Frequently PCs become infected with **Spyware** that collects personal in-formation without letting you know, and without asking for permission. From the websites you visit to usernames and passwords, spyware can put you and your confidential information at risk. In addition to privacy concerns, spyware can hamper your computer's performance. To combat spyware, you might want to consider using the PC safety scan from **Windows Live OneCare**. This scan is a free service and will help check for and remove spyware, adware and other viruses.

Virus Removal Tools:
There are many virus and Trojan removal tools on the internet, including **HiJackThis!, BitDefender,** and **AVG**, to name a few. Personally, I prefer to use Microsoft's free security scanner software (ie; **Microsoft Security Essentials)** and recommend that a PC owner go to the Microsoft website, download and install the scanner on their computer pronto! Before any malware problems occur.

Steps to Take If Your Computer Becomes Infected
Don't panic!
When your computer seems to have a virus it is important to first distinguish between virus symptoms and those that come from corrupted system files. Before suspecting a virus, try to rule out more standard causes - For example: If you just installed new software, try uninstalling it and see if the problems disappear. **Note:** Symptoms such as strange graphics appearing on your screen, unpredictable program behavior, inability to boot, longer-than normal program load times, your computer begins to act strangely, inexplicable changes in file sizes, or unusual sounds may indicate a virus is infecting your system.

If your computer is infected with a virus, you'll want to re-move it as quickly as possible.

Find and Remove Infections con't.

Get the Bugs Out Now!
Here's How to Do It:
1. First Option - Connect to the Internet:
If you can reach a website using your web browser, immediately run an online scan.
1. Go to the Microsoft Safety Scanner webpage to download the scanner.
2. Click '*Download Now*', and then follow the instructions on the screen.

Note: Before you do any repairs, I suggest you disable 'System Restore' to prevent re-infection when you reboot. Once you have run at least three different online anti-threat scans, and have determined that your system has been cleared of all threats, you may then re-enable System Restore.

2. Second Option - Unable to connect to the Internet:
If you can't get online, first try restarting your computer in **safe mode** with **networking** enabled.

Here's How to Do It:
1. Restart your computer.
2. When you see the computer manufacturer's logo, press and hold the F8 key.
3. Advanced users can follow steps in Fourth Option to use a Bootable Rescue Utility.

Find and Remove Infections Con't.

3. On the 'Advanced Boot Options' screen, use the arrow keys to high-light 'Safe Mode with Networking', and then press Enter.
4. Log on to your computer with a user account that has administrator rights.
5. Follow the steps above to run the Microsoft Safety Scanner.

3. Third Option: If you still can't access the Internet after re-starting in safe mode, try resetting your Internet Explorer proxy settings.
Certain strains of malicious software may change Windows Internet Explorer **proxy settings**, and these changes can prevent you from accessing Windows Update or any Microsoft Security sites.
Follow the steps below to reset the proxy settings in the **Windows regis-try** so that you can access the Internet again.
Here's How to Do It:
1. Windows XP, click **Start**, or Windows Vista /Windows 7, 8 click , and then click **Run**.
2. In the **Run** text box, copy (CTRL+C) and paste (CTRL+V) or type the following:
reg add
"HKCU\Software\Microsoft\Windows\CurrentVersion\Internet Set-tings" /v ProxyEnable /t REG_DWORD /d 0 /f
3. Click **OK**.
4. Windows XP, click **Start,** or Windows Vista/Windows 7, 8 click , and then click **Run**.
5. In the **Run** text box, copy (CTRL+C) and paste (CTRL+V) or type the following:
reg delete
"HKCU\Software\Microsoft\Windows\CurrentVersion\Internet Set-tings" /v ProxyServer /f
6. Click **OK**.
7. Next, check whether the problem is fixed. If the problem is fixed, congratulations! You are done.

Find and Remove Infections Con't.

---

4. Fourth Option: Use a Bootable Rescue Utility
Advanced users may just want to make a **Bootable Rescue Disk**
and clean the computer that way.
If you cannot even boot your computer, then you may need to use
a bootable CD/Flash-Drive, also called a bootable disk, to clean
your computer. I know this may sound complicated, but it's really
not. Just remember to create this disk on a computer that is not
infected. Otherwise the files may be corrupted or even possibly
infected.
To do this you should download a good Antivirus Rescue Disk
Utility (There are some free ones on the internet that work pretty
darn well).
Next download an ISO Burning Utility from the internet (again a
free one will work just as well as a paid one.)
Follow the steps to make a Bootable Rescue Disk from the
website you downloaded the Antivirus Rescue Disk Software
from, and the instructions on how to use it to boot your infected
computer..
You can search online to learn more about Bootable Rescue
Utilities, and create one to keep on hand in case your PC does
become infected, and you are not able to boot into it.
**Important: Make sure that you follow the above steps
carefully because serious problems can occur if you
incorrectly modify the registry.**

Note: If you are not sure how to do it yourself, you can have
Microsoft support reset the Internet Explorer proxy settings for
you. To do so, just use the link below to reach Microsoft
webpage, then scroll down to the 'Fix It For Me' section, and
follow the instructions listed there:
http://support.microsoft.com/kb/2289942 - phrss

Security Note: Be sure to update your virus definitions daily,
and scan your computer weekly. If your antivirus software finds a
virus, it will give you the option to repair, delete, or quarantine
the infected file.

Uninstall All Unneeded Applications

Uninstall all applications that you don't use anymore and are no longer needed, and install only the software you know you actually will use frequently.

Note: The more applications you install, the more your Windows system will slow down.

It is not a good idea to install anything and everything you come across unless you know you really need it and is recommended by a source you have come to trust.
When applications and games are installed to a Windows PC, some files are written in the Windows directory structure and dozens (or more) changes are made to the Windows Registry file. Most of these changes are not readily apparent to the user, so proper removal requires *uninstalling* the application through the Control Panel's "Add or Remove Program" or "Programs and Features" icon.

Steps to Uninstall Programs:
1. Click Start, then click 'Control Panel'
2. Next, from the Control Panel click the 'Add or Remove Programs'
3. Scroll through the programs listed, and remove the ones that are no longer needed.
4. Click on the 'Remove' button on the right side ot the page to remove a program

If the program is not listed in the Control Panel use the "uninstall" command provided by the application.
1. Click Start, then click All Programs
2. Locate the program you want to remove
3. Click on the Uninstall command
Simply deleting the entire application directory is not the same as uninstalling, as all the files written to the Windows directory and changes to the Windows Registry file will remain and may be reloaded when the sys-tem is rebooted.
NOTE: Make sure that you do not uninstall any programs that are required by others. e.g. iTunes® will not work if Quicktime® is uninstalled, and many programs rely on other Microsoft programs.

Empty the Recycle Bin

Simply deleting files from the disk doesn't really delete them at all, rather they are moved to a temporary holding area on the hard drive for easy restoration. This area is called the Recycle Bin and is usually displayed on the Desktop. Review the contents before emptying. Once emptied, the space on the hard drive that the data occupied is made available for reuse and the restoration of files emptied from the recycle bin becomes extremely difficult. **Note:** Emptying the Recycle Bin will only speed up your computer if the hard drive is nearly full.

Recycle Bin

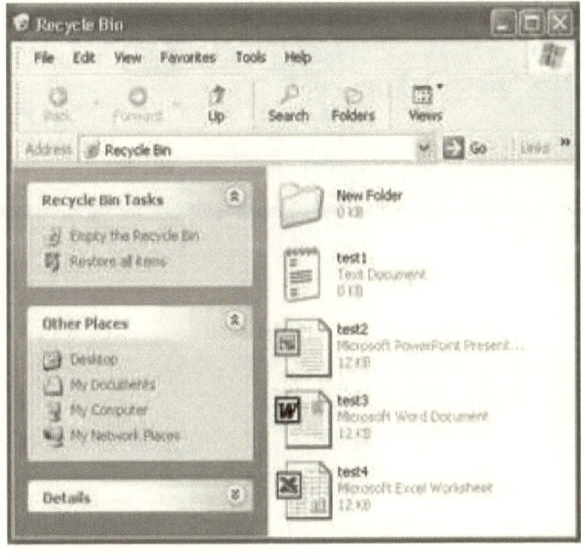

⚠ Your computer is infected!   ⊠

Windows has detected spyware infection!

It is recommended to use special antispyware tools to prevent data loss. Windows will now download and install the most up-to-date antispyware for you.

Click here to protect your computer from spyware!

Chapter 2

Now Keep the Infections Out!

Table of Contents

Is Your PC Protected?

Protect your computer against spyware

Anti-virus (AV) software is an absolute must. It is important to keep it updated regularly as new viruses and e-mail worms are coming out constantly. Install a good AV software on your computer, (preferably one that you can schedule to scan the computer automatically) and keep it up to date. A couple of **free** programs that I use are: **Microsoft Security Essentials** and **Advanced System Care 4**.

There are many from which to choose from, and there are other free AV solutions that do a very good job as well as paid ones. Three popular **free** AV solutions are Avast!, AVG, and Avira AntiVir. All include regular "virus definition" file updates that allow the AV program to detect and protect from the latest virus being released. Note that while installing antivirus software actually slows down your computer, it does not slow it down as much as malware does.

The built-in "Administrator" account

This account is special for a number of reasons, and is disabled by default in **Windows Vista and Windows 7**. Because this account explicitly turns off some important security features (such as Internet Explorer® Protected Mode) as well as UAC, it's a really bad idea to use **Administrator** for anything.

By default **Windows 2000** and **Windows XP** sets you up as an "Administrator". So, I recommend for your own protection, especially when browsing the Internet, you should change the account settings of your computer to a **limited user,** and only log in as an **Administrator** when you need to make changes to Windows such as installing new programs. If you browse the Internet and read your email from a limited user account, you will have much less danger of being infected by a **virus** or a **Trojan.**

"Surfing from a limited account dramatically lowered the attack surface of my system, and it has contributed to my Windows computers never suffering a compromise".

If you computer does become infected while you are using a limited account, don't worry, the virus will only be active until you reboot. Therefore, the virus can only run when you first open an attachment or file, but it cannot modify any of the system settings in the registry or continue to spread and lower security settings on your compromised computer. Surfing the web as a limited user is a lot safer and if your computer gets a virus, you won't have to do any work to clean out the infection from your system. After you reboot the computer it will die and leave no trace of the infection.

Set-Up and Browse From a Limited User Account Con't.

Here's How to Do It:
To change your user account to a limited user:
1. Go to Start, Settings, Control Panel, Users and Passwords, and click on your account name.
2. Next click on Properties.
3. Change the account type to User.
4. Click Ok.

Keep in mind there must be at least one account that has Administrator privileges, so you should not attempt to change the account to User if the name of the account is Administrator. If it is, create a new account with your user name and password. Make sure that the Administrator password is set. It should not be the same as the Limited User account password.

Firewall Protection

Windows Firewall is a software component of Microsoft Windows that provides firewall and packet filtering functions by checking information coming from the Internet or a network, and then either blocks it or allows it to pass through to your computer, depending on your firewall settings.
I recommend using the default firewall settings to help prevent hackers or malicious software (such as worms) from gaining access to your computer through a network or the Internet. Most commercial firewalls include a feature to stop all but authorized applications from sending data to the Internet; this stops malicious code from sending unauthorized communications, and also prevents PCs from being hijacked and used to send spam, participate in distributed denial-of-service attacks and can also help stop your computer from sending malicious software to other computers.

Windows 8 firewall
Even if you think there is nothing on your computer that would interest anyone, a worm could completely disable your computer, or someone could use your computer to help spread worms or viruses to other computers without your knowledge. In some cases, malicious code could indeed switch the firewall off. So keep in mind a Windows Firewall is designed to stop malicious transmissions to the PC, rather than protecting the PC once it's been infected. If malicious code happens to make it past the firewall, it is then the role of anti-virus software to protect the computer.
Windows Firewall is on by default in Windows computers. To make sure it has not been turned off, **follow these steps:**
Here's How to Do It:
1. Open Windows Firewall by clicking the Start button ,
2. Click Control Panel, click Security, and then click Windows Firewall.
3. Click Turn Windows Firewall on or off. If you are prompted for an administrator password or confirmation, type the password or provide confirmation.
4. Next Click On (recommended), and then click OK.

System Restore

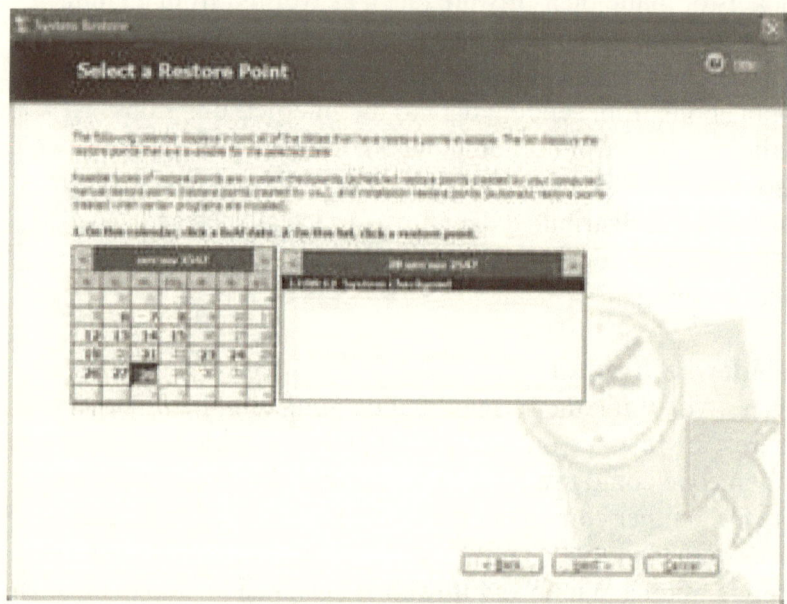

System Restore

System Restore is a component of Microsoft's *Windows Me, Windows XP, Windows Vista, Windows 7 and 8*; but not the *Windows 2000* operating systems. System Restore allows for the rolling back of system files, registry keys, installed programs, etc; to a previous state in the event of system malfunction or failure and certain infections.

System Restore backs up system files of certain extensions (.exe, .dll, etc.) and saves them for later recovery and use. It also backs up the registry and most drivers. Sometimes installing a program or driver can make Windows run slowly or

unpredictably. System Restore can return your PC's system files and programs to a time when everything was working fine, potentially preventing hours of troubleshooting headaches.
Note: System Restore does not affect personal files, such as e-mail, documents, or photos. You can only restore files that you have deleted if you have made backups of those files.

System Restore points are created when the following event occur in Windows:
Automatically every day.
When a new application is installed.
When a new driver is installed.
When you uninstall certain programs.
When new Windows updates are installed.
When you manually create one.
When programs are set to create a new restore point. (This may be done when a program cleans your computer of infections or makes changes to your Windows Registry).

Right before you restore to a previous restore point, System Restore will create a new restore point.

How to Restore a Windows system to a previous State using System Restore

Using System Restore in Windows XP:
Here's How to Do It:
Before you start System Restore, save any open files and close all programs.
1. Open System Restore by clicking the Start button.
2. Click Programs, Accessories and then click System Tools
3. In the list of results, click System Restore.
4. On the Welcome to System Restore page, click Restore my computer to an earlier time, and click Next.
5. Follow the steps in the wizard to choose a restore point and restore your computer. If you're prompted for an administrator password or confirmation, type the password or provide confirmation.
6. On the Select a Restore Point page, click on a **bold** date on the calendar prior to the day of the problem stated.
Note: There may also be a restore point for an earlier time on the same day. Try to use a restore point as close as possible to a time just before the problem started. If the problem persists, an earlier restore point can be used.
7. On the Confirm Restore Point Selection page, click Next.
System Restore restores the previous Windows XP configuration, and then restarts the computer.

Using System Restore in Windows 7 or Vista:
Here's How to Do It:
1. Log on as Administrator.
2. Then from within Windows, you can just type *restore* into the Start menu search box.

3. You'll see System Restore at the top of the start menu.
4. Next you will see a screen where you can choose to roll back the system to the last restore point. Select "Recommended Restore", and just click next, or you can choose a different restore point.
Note: If you are not computer savvy, I recommend you select the "Recommended Restore" option.
5. If you do choose a different restore point, you will see a list of restore points that you can choose from. You may need to install device drivers with this option
.

Windows 8 Users:
1. First go to the Windows 8 Start Screen and type restore point. When the search results appear click on the Settings category.
2. Next click on the option labeled Create a restore point and you will be brought to the System Protection tab of the System Properties control panel.
3. To restore your computer, click on the System Restore button and you will be presented with the main screen for System Restore. Now click on the Next button and you will be shown a list of available restore points that you can restore.
4. Select the restore point you wish to restore by left-clicking on the entry once. This will then make the Scan for affected programs button available. If you click on that button you will be shown a list of programs that will be removed when you perform a restore.
5. If you are okay with the programs that will be deleted, please click on the Close button and then click on the Next button at the restore point selection screen. You will now be at a screen asking if you are sure you wish to perform the restore.
6. If you are sure you wish to continue, please click on the Finish button. System Restore will once again ask if you are sure you wish to continue. If you are sure, please click on the Yes button. System Restore will now reboot your computer and begin the restore process. Please be patient as this can take quite some time.

When the restore point has finished being restored, Windows will start back up and you will be at your login screen or desktop. You will then be shown a confirmation box
Your computer has now been restored back to the selected point in time.

Disabling System Restore
Disabling System Protection will delete all existing restore points.

Windows XP Users
Here's How to Do It:
1. Right-click the **My Computer** icon on the Desktop and click **Proper-ties**. 2. Click the **System Restore** tab. 3. Put a check mark next to **T urn off System Restore on All Drives**. 4. Click **OK**. 5. Click **Yes** when prompted to restart.
Note: To re-enable the System Restore Utility, follow the steps above, but remove the check mark next to **Turn off System Restore on All Drives**

Windows Vista
Here's How to Do It:
1. Click the Start button. 2. Click Control Panel. 3. Click System and Maintenance. 4. Click System. 5. In the left pane, click System Protection. If prompted, enter your Ad-ministrator password or click Continue. 6. Uncheck the box next to the disk on which you wish to disable System Restore
7. Click **OK**.

Note: To re-enable the System Restore Utility, follow the steps above, but check the box next to the disk on which you wish to enable System Restore.

**Instructions for Windows XP, Vista Windows 7 and 8
Windows XP:**

1. You may want to perform an in-place upgrade/ repair installation if your installation of Windows XP must be repaired and if one of the following conditions is true:
2. You cannot start Windows XP in safe mode.
3. You cannot start Windows XP after you install a
4. Microsoft software update.
5. There is a registry problem that cannot be solved by using other tools such as System Restore.
6. You must apply default (file and registry) permissions to your Windows XP installation. This condition can occur if program files are missing or damaged after you make changes or updates to your computer or pro-grams.
7. You must register COM components and Windows File Protection (WFP) files. This condition occurs because of missing or damaged system files.
8. You must use the Windows Setup program to enumerate Plug and Play devices again. This includes the hardware abstraction layer (HAL).

Go to Microsoft/support for Step-by-Step Instructions:

Important: If you are not comfortable trying to reinstall or repair the Windows operating system, you might want to contact your computer manufacturer for help or bring your computer to a professional repair shop.

Reinstalling the Windows operating system or performing an in-place up-grade of your operating system is an extreme troubleshooting step that you should only take if you fully understand the ramifications and risks involved. If you decide to take this step, make sure that you have the original Windows XP installation media and product key that was included with your operating system.

Reinstall Windows XP

To reinstall Windows XP, try either of the following methods. If the first method does not work, try the second.

Here's How to Do It: Note You may want to disconnect from the Internet during the installation. This helps protect you from malicious users.

Method 1: Start the reinstallation from Windows XP

To reinstall Windows XP by using Windows XP CD, follow these steps:

1. Start your computer.
2. Insert the Windows XP CD in your computer's CD drive or DVD drive.
3. On the Welcome to Windows XP page, click **Install Windows XP**.
4. On the Welcome to Windows Setup page, click **Upgrade (Recommended)** in the **Installation Type** box (if it is not already selected), and then click **Next**.

5. On the License Agreement page, click **I accept this agreement**, and then click **Next**.
6. On the Your Product Key page, type the 25-character product key in the **Product key** boxes, and then click **Next**.
7. On the Get Updated Setup Files page, select the option that you want, and then click **Next**.
8. Follow the instructions that appear on the screen to reinstall Windows XP.
If you received an error or if the re installation did not finish, try method 2.

Method 2: Repair install of Windows XP by starting your computer from the Windows XP CD
Note If Windows XP was pre-installed on your computer, you may need the installation CD to reinstall. Contact your computer manufacturer to make sure that you have the installation CD for a repair installation. To reinstall Windows XP by starting your computer from the Windows XP CD, follow these steps:
Here's How to Do It:
1. Insert the Windows XP CD into your computer's CD drive or DVD drive, and then restart your computer.
2. When you receive the "Press any key to boot from CD" message on the screen, press a key to start your computer from the Windows XP CD.

3. The following message on the Welcome to Setup screen will appear:

"This portion of the Setup program prepares Microsoft Windows XP to run on your computer: To setup Windows XP now, press ENTER. To repair a Windows XP installation by using Recovery Console, press R. To quit Setup without installing Windows XP, press F3".

4. Press **ENTER** to set up Windows XP.

5. On the **Windows XP Licensing Agreement** screen, press **F8** to agree to the license agreement.

6. Make sure that your current installation of Windows XP is selected in the box, and then press **R** to repair Windows XP.

7. Follow the instructions that appear on the screen to reinstall Windows XP. After you repair Windows XP, you may have to reactivate your copy of Windows XP.

After you reinstall Windows XP

After you finish the re-installation, complete the following final tasks. **Note** It is recommended that you enable the firewall in Internet Explorer at this time.

1. Reinstall Windows XP Service Pack 2

If Windows XP Service Pack 2 (SP2) was installed on your computer before you reinstalled Windows XP, you must reinstall SP2. If you did not already reinstall SP2 with the Windows XP in the previous section, use one of the following methods to reinstall SP2 now.

Method 1: Obtain the service pack CD and reinstall the service pack after you reinstall Windows XP.

Method 2: Download the service pack from microsoft after you reinstall Windows XP

2. Reinstall all updates to Windows

After you reinstall Windows XP, you must reinstall all updates to Win-dows also. To reinstall Windows updates, visit the following Microsoft Web site: http://update.microsoft.com

3. Reinstall Drivers and Software Programs

Drivers such as sound, network, and device drivers may need to be reinstalled. Also certain software applications will need to be reinstalled.

Reinstall Operating System - Windows 7:
Here's How to Do It:

There are two options to choose from during the Windows 7 installation process:

1. Upgrade. This option replaces your current version of Windows with Windows7, and keeps your files, settings, and programs in place on your computer.

2. **Custom**. This option replaces your current version of Windows with Windows 7, but doesn't preserve your files, settings, and programs. It's sometimes referred to as a *clean installation* for that reason.

NOTE: If Windows7 doesn't run at all, you can reinstall Windows using your original Windows 7 installation disc. To do this, follow the instructions in "Using the Custom installation option and formatting the hard disk".

Windows 7 Advanced Recovery Method

The advanced methods available in Recovery in Control Panel can return Windows to a usable state if it's badly damaged.

You can reinstall Windows 7 using 'Recovery' in the Control Panel, under 'Advanced Recovery Methods'. This method reinstalls Windows 7, either from a recovery image provided by your computer manufacturer, or from your original Windows 7 installation files. You need to reinstall all of the programs that you added, and restore all of your files from a backup. Thre are two methods for doing this.

The first method uses a type of backup called a *system image*, which you need to have created earlier. The second method reinstalls Windows, either from a *recovery image* provided by your computer manufacturer, or from the original Windows installation files.

How to access advanced recovery methods- Windows 7
Here's How to Do It:
1. Open Recovery by clicking the Start button, and then click Control Panel.
2. In the search box, type recovery, and then click Recovery.
3. Click Advanced Recovery Methods.

Windows 8 clean install process
There are really four basic steps here:
1. Insert the Windows 8 DVD into your optical drive, or plug into a free USB port the flash drive with the Windows 8 installation files on it, and then turn on or restart the computer.
2. Watch for a Press any key to boot from CD or DVD... message (shown above) if you're booting from a disc, or a Press any key to boot from external device... message if you're booting from a flash drive or other USB device.
3. Press a key to force your computer to boot from either the Windows 8 DVD or a flash drive with the Windows 8 installation files on it.
If you don't press a key to force the boot from the external drive or DVD disc, your computer will try to boot from the next device listed in the boot order in BIOS, probably your hard drive.
4. Follow onscreen instructions to install Windows 8.

Reinstall Operation System - Windows Vista:
If you want to reinstall Windows Vista by performing a clean installation - possibly to restore the default Windows settings.
Here's How to Do It:
1. Turn on your computer and insert the Windows Vista DVD or CD.
2. On the Install Windows page, follow any instructions that might ap-pear, and then click Install now.
3. On the Get important updates for installation page, we recommend getting the latest updates to help ensure a successful installation and to help protect your computer against security threats. You will need an Internet connection to get installation updates.
4. On the **'Type your product key for activation'** page, type your 25-character product key to help avoid problems during activation.
5. On the **'Please read the license terms'** page, click I accept the license terms.
6. Follow the instructions on each page. On the **'Which type of installation do you want?'** page, click Custom.
7. On the **'Where do you want to install Windows?'** page, select the partition where you want to install Windows.
8. Click Next to begin the installation. You might see a compatibility re-port.
9. Follow the instructions.

ADVANCED OPTIONS

Chapter 3

Advanced Tips & Tactics

NOTE: THE FOLLOWING ADVANCED TIPS AND TACTICS ARE RECOMMENDED FOR ADVANCED USERS

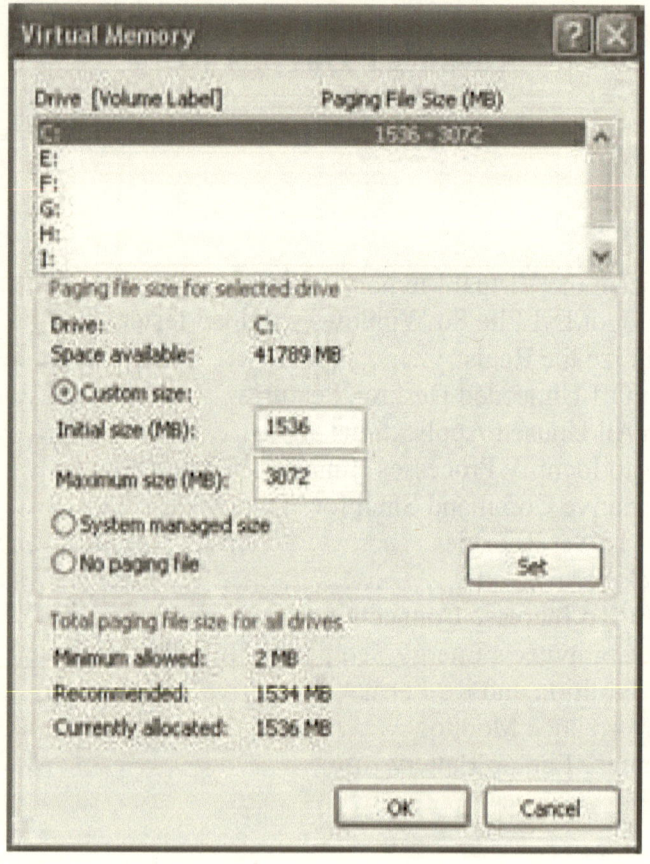

Pagefile.sys is your Windows virtual memory swap file. **Virtual memory** is simulated RAM. When you have used up all of your *RAM,* your computer will shift data to an empty space on the hard drive. The computer swaps data to the hard disk and back to your RAM as needed. When you increase your virtual memory you are increasing the empty space that is reserved for your RAM overflow. Also having enough available space is absolutely necessary for your virtual memory and RAM to function properly.

These files (depending on Windows version installed) are hidden and are usually located on the Windows drive (usually "C:") If there is a second physical hard drive in the system, consider moving to the secondary drive. Ideally, these files work best when located on the fastest and largest (in terms of free space) drive in the system.

A very large cache of pagefile.sys may slow down your system.

Moving pagefile.sys - Windows 7

Here's How to Do It:

1. Right click on "**My Computer**" or the "**Computer**" item in your start menu and click on properties.

2. In Windows 7 click on the **Advanced system settings link**.

3. Click on the **Advanced** tab.

4. In the box labeled "Performance", click on the **Settings** button.

5. Click on the **Advanced** tab in the resulting dialog.:

6. Next, you'll see the "Virtual memory" section showing how much space has been set aside for your paging files.

7. Click on Change.

Steps to remove pagefile.sys in windows 8

1. Go to Computer Properties.

2. Now, Go to Advanced System Settings.

3. Under the Advanced tab select the Performance.

4. Again in the Performance Options select the Advanced tab.ce Settings option.

5. Click on the Change button.

6. In the Virtual Memory window uncheck the Automatically manage paging file size for all drives option.

7. Select the No paging file radio button and click Set then press OK.

8. To apply these settings finally reboot your system

After the computer restarts you will be free from pagefile.sys.

Note: The default is to have the system manage your paging file size for you, and most likely placed the entire file on the C: drive.

To change that:

1. Uncheck the "Automatically manage paging file size for all drives" set-ting (Win 7).

2. Click on the drive you want to move pagefile.sys **to**

3. Click on **System Managed Size**

4. Click **Set**

5. lick on the drive currently holding pagefile.sys (probably C:)

6. Click on **No paging file**

7. Click **Set**

8. Click on **OK**

Moving pagefile.sys - Windows XP

Here's How to Do It:

1. Click Start, and then click **Control Panel**. 2. Click **Performance and Maintenance**, and then click System. 3. On the Advanced tab, under Performance, click **Settings**. 4. On the Advanced tab, under **Virtual memory**, click Change. 5. Under **Drive [Volume Label]**, click the drive that contains the paging file that you wants to change. 6. Under **Paging file size** for selected drive, click to **Custom size** check box. You can enter the amount of memory you would like to reserve for Virtual memory by entering the initial and maximum size.

7. Once you have completed all of this check the Custom Size checkbox. Now you are able to input how much memory you want to save for virtual memory. There will be two fields there, the first one is called initial and the other is called maximum. If you want the best performance out of your machine you should set these the same as each other.

8. Click Set; when you are prompted to restart the computer, click Yes. Special Note: You should choose the same amount for the initial size and maximum size. This will stop your CPU from constantly changing the paging file.
This setting will help your gaming process by speeding up your computer.

HOT TIP: To stop your CPU from constantly changing the paging file, set the initial and maximum size to the same value. For example, 500 and 500. The value should be at least 1.5 times more than your physical RAM. If your computer has 512MB of RAM increase the virtual memory paging file to 1.5*512= 768 Remember to choose the drive you would like to use to increase the virtual memory. In most cases it usually your C: Drive. You can set the initial size and maximum size after clicking the Custom size check box. Remember it's better to keep the Virtual memory values the same.

NOTE: When your computer consumes your computer's hard drive and uses it as RAM, it is referred to as **thrashing.** Thrashing is bad for your computer and buying a RAM (it's not that expensive) is much more worthwhile.

EXAMPLE BOOT.INI FILE

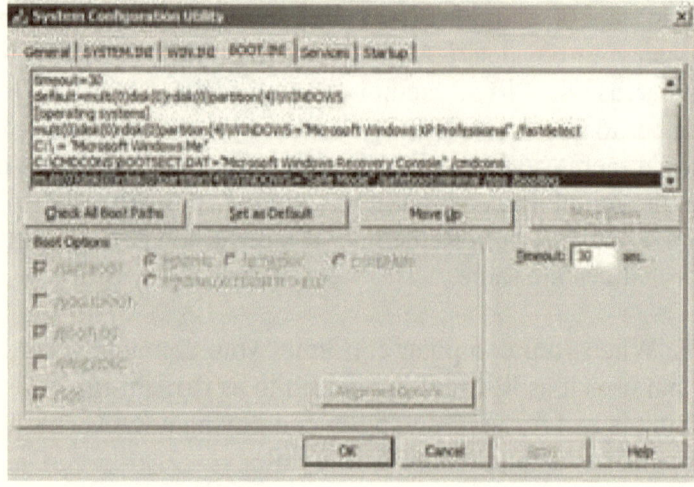

Make Windows Boot Faster by Editing Boot.ini File
In **earlier versions** of Windows, **boot.ini** was a system file that
contained information about the Windows operating systems
installed on the computer. This information was displayed during
the startup process when you turned on your computer. It was
most useful in multiboot configurations, or for advanced users or
administrators who needed to customize how Windows started.
In **Windows 7** and **8** the boot.ini file has been replaced with Boot
Configuration Data (BCD). This file is more versatile than
boot.ini, and it can apply to computer platforms that use means
other than basic in-put/output system (BIOS) to start the
computer.
If you need to make changes to BCD, such as removing entries
from the list of displayed operating systems, use the command
line tool Bcdedit, an advanced tool intended for administrators
and IT professionals. For technical information about Bcdedit, go
to the **Microsoft website for IT professionals**.

Editing the Boot.INI File:
The **Boot.ini** is a text file always found at the system root,
usually at *C:\Boot.ini*, and is one of the very first files windows
refer during the boot process. It's a hidden read-only file, so if
you don't see it in your *C:* you can enable viewing of system and
hidden files on your computer by going to Tools > Folder
Options > View > advanced options uncheck 'Hide extensions
for known file types" and select "show hidden files and fold-ers"
radio button. After enabling 'viewing of hidden files and folders'
Boot.ini will now be visible at c:\ (or whatever your computers
system partition is.)

Note*: Before you open up or edit the* **Boot.ini** *file it would be
wise to copy and paste it elsewhere in the drive to serve as a
backup, in case something goes wrong you will have a backup
copy to replace it.*

Edit Boot.INI File So Windows Will Load Faster con't.

There are two things that can be tweaked in the Boot.ini file to considerably boost windows start up time.
Change Time-Out so Windows will load faster
Here's How to Do It:
1. Click Start, then Run.
2. Type in 'msconfig' and press enter.
3. Click on the BOOT.INI tab at the top.
4. Over to the right there will be a box labeled Timeout with 30 in it. Change the 30 to a 3.

NOTE: Timeout=30" this tells windows how many seconds it has to wait before booting the default operating system.

Secondly, adding a switch called **/noguiboot** removes the default windows loading animation when windows boots up and thus saves consider-able time.
This can be done by adding the switch next to the /fast detect switch. So "WINDOWS=" Microsoft Windows XP Professional "/fastdetect" be-comes "WINDOWS=" Microsoft Windows XP Professional "/fastdetect /noguiboot".

NOTE: Leave a single space between the t of fast detect and / of noguiboot.

Save the Boot.ini file and reboot the system and enjoy the faster boot up time. If something doesn't happen as expected, not to worry, you always have the saved copy of the original Boot.ini file. Just replace the edited one with the original.

The registry is vital to Windows' operation, so if you are not familiar with the registry, do not try to edit it manually. You can remove or correct registry errors that may cause your computer to crash, and you can optimize the registry's organization to speed it up with a third-party application. There are many software programs to choose from, that you can find and use to clean out unused DLL files from your Windows\System directory.

You can go to: http://www.microsoft.com to get and run the latest version of Microsoft's RegClean. This program will likely do the best job of cleaning the registry since it is written by Microsoft for their own operating system.

Here's How to Do It Manually:
Note: Most of the steps below use programs you can download for free from the Internet, but some require you to purchase them.
1. First, Backup your Registry in case you need to restore your Registry later if problems occur.
2. The root directory of your hard drive contains a lot of files that are necessary, and you must be careful when deleting them. However, removing some of them can help to speed up your computer.
3. Be careful when doing this, but you should be able to restore these files by booting to a boot disk and restoring the files if necessary.

Note: The files listed below should **not** be deleted:
c:\command.com c:\autoexec.bat c:\config.sys c:\msdos.sys
c:\io.sys c:\drvspace.bin c:\dblspace.bin c:\suhdlog.dat
c:\bootsect.dos

Autoexec.bat works kind of like your startup folder, except these programs start up even before you get into Windows. Aside from a virus scanning program, you most likely do not need any of the files here.

To find out
Here's How to Do It:
1. Edit the file in Windows by right clicking on it and going to Edit.
2. Type **REM** in front of each line, which will prevent that line from being executed. This is simple to do and won't restore it to its original state! If a problem exists, boot to a floppy disk. Then enter the following command:
edit c:\autoexec.bat
3. Then delete the REM in front of the line or lines that may be causing the problem, save the file, and restart. CD-ROM and sound card support are provided through Windows, so you can remove any lines related to these hardware devices.

If you have Norton Utilities, run Norton WinDoctor to get rid of some of the quick, easy to fix registry errors. Run Norton Optimization Wizard to optimize your registry, optimize your swap file, and optimize your file structure with Speed Disk (an enhanced defrag utility). You may want to run ScanDisk or Norton Disk Doctor now. Let WinDoctor repair all er-rors automatically.
Restart your computer to make sure everything is still running okay. After completing all of these steps, you should have a fast and reliable machine once again.

NOTE: I **Do Not** recommend tinkering with the registry files. Such activities can be detrimental to your computer and should only be attempted by properly trained professionals.

Registry Editor

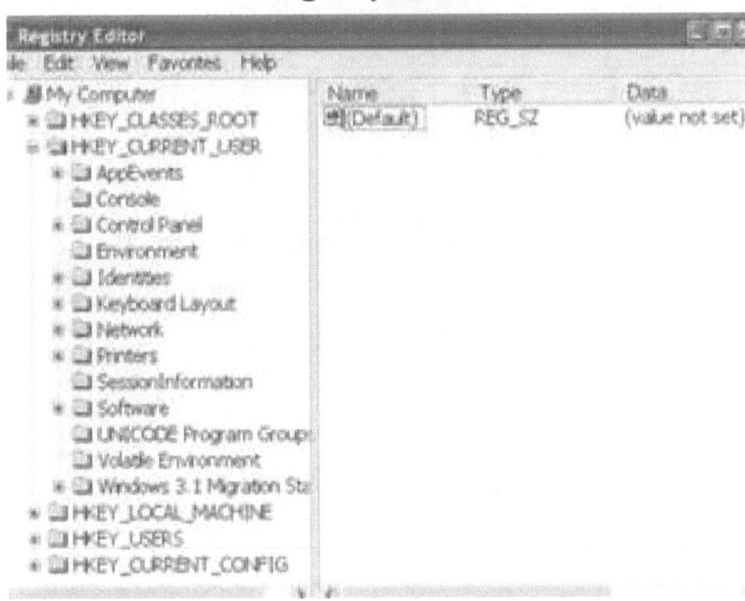

Blank Screen Desktop

Turn Off Unneeded Desktop Features

Turn off unneeded **Desktop Features** that try to make things look better, like the fancy rounded window corners, the way the menus fade in and out, and the 3-D button styles on modern Desktops can overwhelm older machines. You can turn off these 'appearance only' enhancements

Here's How to Do It - Windows XP:
1. Right click on My Computer, and choose the Properties option.
2. Then choose the Advanced tab, and click the Settings button under the Performance section.
3. In the Performance Options dialogue that comes up, go to the Visual Effects tab, and choose "Adjust for best performance". You can also try the "Custom" option, and turn on and off individual settings to see which ones will work without slowing your machine down.

Here's How to Do It - Vista:
1. Click the Start button, then Control Panel, then choose System and Maintenance, then Performance Information and Tools.
2. Click Adjust visual effects. If you are prompted for an administrator password or confirmation, type the password or provide confirmation.
3. Click the Visual Effects tab, and choose "Adjust for best performance". You can also try the "Custom" option, and turn on and off individual set-tings to see which ones will work without slowing your machine down.

Here's How to Do It - Windows 7:
1. Click the Start button, then Control Panel, and then System and Security.
2. Look for System, click on it and then Advanced system settings. From here you can make sure you're on the Advanced tab and click on Settings under Performance.
3. You can also choose Adjust for best performance or choose Custom if you'd like to compromise between fancy visuals and performance.

Disable Windows 8 metro style desktop
The new Metro Style desktop is the biggest feature offered by **Windows 8**. It is a bit difficult for the traditional windows users to get used to it especially the desktop users. If you are facing difficulties navigating through it, disabling it might be an option. Follow the steps below to learn how to disable Metro Desktop.
1. In the Metro Start Menu, click on the lower left corner. When the Start menu pops up. Click Search.
2. Next in the Apps Search Box, type regedit and press enter.
3. The Registry Editor opens. Navigate to HKEY_CURRENT_USER\Software\Microsoft\Windows\CurrentVersion\Explorer. The name value pairs will be displayed.
4. Right click on RPEnabled and select Modify.
5. Changing the value to 0 will disable the Metro style desktop. Click OK when done.

Stop All Unused Applications

The Taskbar is on the bottom edge of the screen (unless relocated by the user). In the right side of the Taskbar appears a group of small icons, collectively named the "system tray". Each of these icons represents a pro-gram on your computer that has been at least partially started or is running "in the background". Regardless of state, each causes a reduction of available memory and processing power, or resources. Closing, exiting or canceling any unused icon returns those resources to the system, and becomes available for use by the application(s) started specifically by the user.

Here's How to Do It:
1. Go to your task manager and click on the Process tab.
2. End all process that you can.
Note: Read the next section **(How to Identify Processes Running on Your PC),** to find out which ones are safe to shut down.
A utility called **Process Explorer** can be used to list all programs running on your Windows system. It is more comprehensive than the Task Manager, and hovering your mouse pointer over any program name will tell you what it is about.

Disable any programs you do not want load automatically.
Note: Do not disable processes if you are unsure, as some processes are necessary for your computer to function normally.
You can also download **StartUpCPL,** then install the software you have just downloaded. Next, open control panel, select **Start up.**

A useful program called "Game Booster" by the people who wrote the Advanced SystemCare V3 software will temporarily disable unnecessary background processes and boost performance on your computer when you are actively using only one program; such as a game program or video editing software. When you are finished, you can resume "normal mode" and all the background processes will be reloaded.

Task Manager

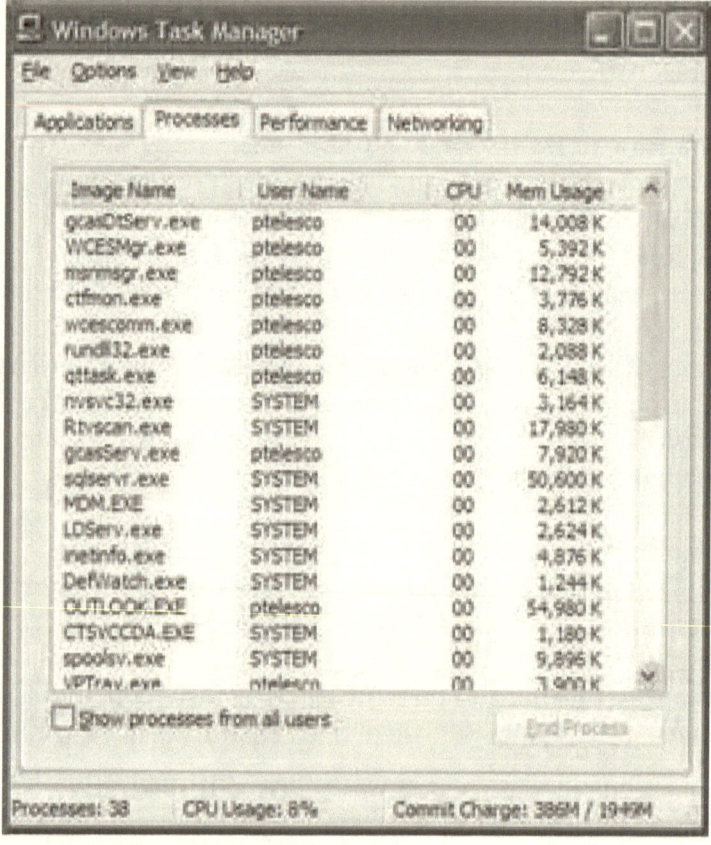

Task Manager Processes – Which Ones Are Safe to Shut-Down?

Task Manager is a windows utility that identifies all the current programs running on the computer. It is launched by either right clicking the Taskbar, or by pressing Ctrl-Alt-Del keys at the same time. The Task Manager is used to end programs that are no longer needed or responding well, and to see how much CPU time and memory programs are using.

Processes are programs that are running on your system: To view these programs bring up the Task Manager, then click the **'Process'** tab.

Note: Some programs are being used by your system, and the software that you have installed on your PC is using the others. From the 'Task manager' you can shutdown, or change the 'priority' of certain processes running on your computer. Terminating services in the Task Manager will only affect the system until you reboot it. So if you want to permanently stop a process, it's better to change their boot settings in the 'Computer Management' console from the 'Control Panel'.
You can do this by launching **"Services"** from the Windows Control Panel → **'Administrative Tools'** or by typing **"Services.msc"** in the **Run** command of the Start menu.

In the recesses of your computer, there can be 20-30 invisible processes running silently in the background. Some processes hog system resources, turning your PC into a sluggish computer. Worse yet, there is a possibility that other processes harbor spyware and Trojans - violating your privacy and giving hackers free reign on your computer. (Most viruses do not run as processes).

Note: Killing certain processes will activate the 'NT **authority protection',** which will shut the computer down within 60 seconds.

There are some processes running on your computer that cannot be shut down and you will see a **"This is a critical system process and cannot be ended"** message if you attempt to do so. Also if you were to end a process required by windows, this is what will happen:

1. Windows will hang or

The process will restart.

2. If any other process is ended:

The program running that process will end or,

If it is a multi-process program, it will lose that functionality or restart the process.

Important: If you are not sure about what you are doing, you should check program dependencies, make sure you have made a *'system restore'* point, backup the registry and make a note of what you changed.

How to Identify Processes:

To see what a process does and find out which processes are safe to shut-down or have been installed as spyware, check out some of the various resources online to help you identify the processes running on your computer, and determine if your computer is infected with spyware, adware or viruses due to some of those programs.

There are many various processes that can run in the background of a system, and too many to list here. For a comprehensive list of processes running on your computer go to one of the resources listed below:

http://www.tasklist.org/
http://www.liutilities.com/products/wintaskspro/processlibrary/

There you can also enter the name of a particular *'Process'* into the site's Find field, press **ENTER**, and see what it says.
If you prefer, you can also upload your Task Manager File To:
http://www.checkprocesses.com/

CheckProcesses.com provides you with a quick and easy way for checking process details from windows task manager. Their OCR service finds the process names, and provides you a list with detailed information relating to each process.

How To Do It: Windows XP/Vista/Win7. 8
1. Click Start
2. From Start Menu click All programs
3. Then click Accessories
4. Click System Tools
5. Select "System Information"
6. Once running expand the 'Software Information' section by clicking on the + symbol in the tree diagram on left
7. Select "Running Tasks"
8. Then click File | Export
9. Save file as: .jpg, .jpeg, .png, .gif
10. Go to: http://www.checkprocesses.com/ and submit file as instructed.

Alternative Command Shell for Windows

Windows PowerShell is an extensible command-line shell and associated scripting language from Microsoft. Windows PowerShell integrates with the Microsoft .NET Framework and provides an environment for execution of cmdlets, which are specialized .NET classes implementing a particular operation, scripts, which are composition of cmdlets along with imperative logic, executables, which are standalone applications, or by instantiating regular .NET classes.

Windows shell is by default explorer.exe. However there are more options available now for Windows scripting. You can run an alternate Windows shell such as PowerShell, Cygwin, Emerge Desktop and SharpE to save on RAM usage and boost performance.

Many — if not most — shell replacements offer a trimmed interface that frees up valuable resources that would otherwise be hogged by a bloated transparency process. Many of these shells come from the open source world, namely from the same people who create similar desktop environments for Linux. Many Linux distributions boast a remarkably frugal idle resource requirement without sacrificing the gloss and shine that com-mercial operating systems are known for. You can search 'Alternative Command Shell for Windows' online to find out more about changing the Windows operating environment to match something more suited to your needs

Note: Although more expensive, installing additional RAM is a better option. Running an alternate shell is a compatibility risk as many proprietary Microsoft programs, such as their latest game or Visual Studio, may not function properly on a third-party shell. EXAMPLE: **Cairo – Windows** Shell **Alternative**

TASK MANAGER PRIORITIES

services.exe	00	3,500 k
Skype.exe	00	21,424 K
smss.exe	00	412 K
spoolsv.exe	00	4,940 K
svchost.exe	00	3,716 K
svchost.exe	00	4,516 K
svchost.exe	00	20,560 K
svchost.exe	00	4,200 K
svchost.exe	00	3,772 K
svchost.exe	00	3,876 K
svchost.exe	00	7,368 K
System	00	240 K
System Idle Process	99	28 K

Context menu:
- End Process
- End Process Tree
- Debug
- Set Priority ▶
- Set Affinity...

Set Priority submenu:
- Realtime
- High
- ■ AboveNormal
- Normal
- BelowNormal
- Low

☐ Show processes from all users

End Pro...

How to Set Priorities

The higher (or lower) you set a program's **'priority'**, the more (or fewer) system resources will be allocated to it, so it will run faster (or slower) than it did before. **"Low"**, for example, is fine for a program running in background that you do not need to have finish up soon, so that more resources are freed up. **"Realtime"** is best for something that absolutely has to have maximum resources right now!

Set priority for Explorer.exe to Realtime for increased speed. Here's How to Do It:
1. Open Task Manager by pressing Control (ctrl) Alt Delete (del) at the same time.
2. Once Task Manager opens, click the process's tab.
3. Now find explorer.exe, right click it, and set the priority to realtime.

This makes your computer focus on explorer.exe, which is your task bar and visual objects. Use this method if you want to keep your visual styles (or you are using a transformation pack). This method greatly increases speed and if you are noticing that other programs that you use a lot are slow, you can set their priority to either high or above normal.

Important: If you have 2 process's on high at the same time, your computer will be unstable, and might crash.

NOTE: For users without Admin password you will not be able to modify the value to realtime, if you aren't on an admin account, or you have insufficient privileges, then the best you can do, is set to high.

Permission

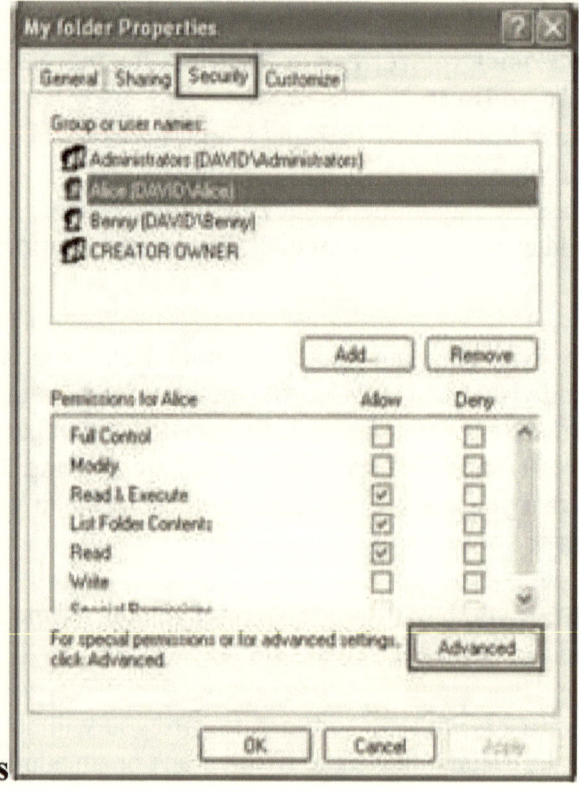

s

Check if other programs are trying to access the internet:
Often your connection speed is slow because other programs are
using it. Follow the steps below to test if other programs, such as
anti-virus and other **updates,** are accessing the Internet without
your knowing.

Here's How to Do It:
1. Click Start, Click Run. Type "cmd" (without quotes).
2. On the command screen type "netstat -b 5 > activity.txt".
3. After a minute or so, hold down Ctrl and press C. This has
created a file with a list of all programs using your Internet
connection.
4. Type activity.txt to open the file and view the program list.

How to Block full Internet Access to a Program

Here's How to Do It:
1. To completely block a program's internet access, search
"Firewall" in the start menu and look for "Windows Firewall
with Advanced Security" and choose it. 2. Select **"Inbound
Rules"** (you might have to wait a second for the pro-grams to
appear), 3. Next, you should see a list of programs on your computer. Choose the one you want to block and right-click it (if you
see two copies of the same program, do this to both of them).
4. Then select "Properties". Under "General" in the pop-up
window, click the box under "action" marked "Block the
Connections" (make sure you do this to both of the programs). 5.
Now choose "Outbound rules" in the left panel. Go to
Action>New rule. In the new window, choose "Program", then
specify the program you want to block and click next.

THE NEED FOR SPEED!

No matter how fast your Internet connection is, there are times when things will slow down to a crawl. ***A poorly running PC can dramatically slow down even the fastest network connection.*** The type of Internet connection you use is the most important factor in determining your connection speed. There are many different ways to connect to the Internet. The three most common ways to connect to the Internet from home are **dial-up, DSL**, and **cable**. With a dial-up connection, the Internet user can connect to the Internet via his or telephone line and an Internet service provider. This method of connecting to the Internet is generally considered the cheapest, but it is also provides the user with the slowest overall connection speeds. However, it may suit the purposes of the occasional Internet user without a need for a fast or consistent connection.
Broadband connections offer another way to connect to the Internet. In this category are **cable** and **DSL** connections. With a cable connection, the user must subscribe to a cable-television/Internet service. These connections are typically very fast, offering speeds upwards of 70 times faster than dial-up connections. They also allow the user to stay connected to the Internet at all times; the user need only open a browser window to access the Internet, as there is no log-on process to complete.

NOTE: If you have a choice, cable is usually the fastest, but both DSL and cable are faster than dial-up.

In addition to broadband and dial-up services, web users are now able to connect to the Internet wirelessly, accessing the web without wires or cables of any type. Wireless technology allows users to have mobile connections, accessing the web (with some limitations) where and when they need to. This can be accomplished via public Wi-Fi networks, cellular services, and Wimax — a somewhat newer type of wireless service. These technologies vary in terms of connectivity, reliability, and cost, but they all allow users to connect whether they are at home, school, work, or on the road.

Satellite Internet service is another form of high-speed Internet connection. It employs telecommunications satellites to allow users to connect to the Internet. Typically, such connections are most popular in areas in which cable and DSL connections are either una-vailable or unreliable. However, satellite connections are usually slower than cable and DSL connections. Also, they often experience high net-work latency because of delays in data transmission, and this can lead to a rather lethargic performance, especially when it comes to gaming and downloading.

How To Increase Internet Connection Speed: Windows XP QoS Packet Scheduler is a method of network bandwidth management that can monitor the importance of data packets and depending upon the priority of the packet, give it higher or lower priority or bandwidth levels. The problem is, XP seems to want to reserve 20% of the bandwidth for itself. Even with QoS disabled, even when this item is disabled. So why not use it to your advantage.

If you have Windows XP, try this. Everyone that has tried it says it works. It's not very useful unless you're using apps which are QoS-aware or run-ning a server, so you can gain some network overhead back by turning it off. This tweak is a pretty common one most old-school users of XP already know – it's not at all detrimental and you can immediately gain 20% of your bandwidth back, increasing Internet performance significantly.

Note: The following steps will not work on *XP Home Edition*. This tip is designed for increased broadband speed in Windows XP and Vista, but it should work for 56k modems too.

Here's How to Do It:
1. Make sure you're logged on as actually "Administrator". **Note: Do Not log on with any account that just has administrator privileges.**
2. Click Start > Run > type gpedit.msc (not available in home version).
3. Expand the Local Computer Policy branch.
4. Expand the Administrative Templates branch.
5. Expand the Network branch.

6. Highlight the "QoS Packet Scheduler" in left window.
7. In right window double click the "limit reservable bandwidth" setting.
8. On setting tab check the ENABLED item.
9. Where it says "Bandwidth limit %" change it to read 0 (ZERO).
10. Close gpedit.msc.
On some systems the effect is immediate, but others will need to re-boot.

Vista Internet Speed Tweak 1:
In Vista, Microsoft implemented *IPv6,* and upon install it is set as the default. The sad part is that it simply doesn't work well with devices that still utilize the *IPv4* protocol, and to assume that most home networks are fully upgraded to the *IPv6* protocol is a bad approach to setting defaults.
Many people upgrade their PCs and laptops long before they consider replacing that old outdated router. So, when they bring home a new PC or laptop with Vista installed they soon discover that the computer and the router is not communicating.
So, if you happen to find yourself in this situation – the first thing you should do is to disable **IPv6** so that you can at least *get on* the Internet, after doing so, you can then get started *speeding up* your Internet connection.

Here's How to Do It:
1. First, go to *Start -> Network -> Network and Sharing Center,* and then click on *"Manage Network Connections."* In this screen, it's likely you'll have a wireless connection displaying that it can't connect to any network.

2. Right-click on that icon and select "Properties." Note that both **IPv6** and **IPv4** enabled.

3. Next, uncheck the box for **IPv6** and click "OK." You'll need to reboot your computer. 4. If the protocol incompatibility was your problem (*and very likely it was*), you'll find that your computer can now communicate fine with the router.

Note: Another complication Microsoft introduced into Vista, just to encourage you that much more to upgrade your router – it's something called **"autotuning,"** and it's also the next Vista tweak.

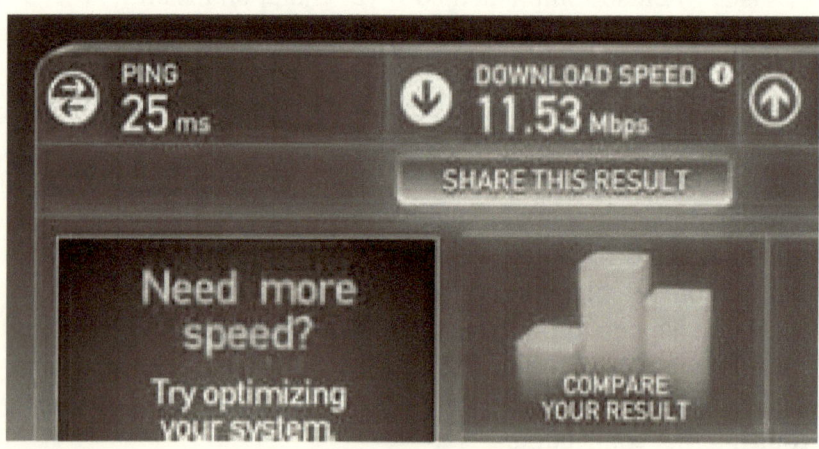

Vista Connection Speed Tweak #2 – Autotuning
Here is another case where the cutting edge technological advances being enabled on Microsoft's operating system by default is a recipe for disaster for users who have older networks and older network devices (specifically older routers). Vista comes installed and enabled with something called:
"Receive Window Auto-Tuning."

On advanced networks, it's actually a good technology where the transfer of data is monitored and Vista automatically "tunes" the TCP window field to optimize packet transfer. Older routers simply do not respond well when it comes to that kind of window resizing. This can be trouble for home users who don't know what a packet of data is.
Consequently, there's a way for you, the home user, to turn this default feature off as well.

Here's How to Do It:
1. First, click on *"Start"* and type **"cmd"** and right-click on the command icon. You'll see the following window:

2. Next click on *"Run as Administrator."* Then, in the command box, type **"netsh interface tcp set global autotuning=disabled"** which will disable autotuning.

3. Now that you've got your new Vista finally communicating with your router (hopefully), you're ready to tweak Vista even more in order to dramatically boost the Internet speed.

Vista Speed Tweak #3 – Take Back Your Bandwidth

Another unnecessary default setting that Vista (and actually XP as well) comes with is a 20% "reserve" of your available bandwidth in order to accommodate certain applications like Windows Update. With this tweak you can immediately gain 20% of your bandwidth back, increasing Internet performance significantly.

This is called the QoS Reserve Bandwidth Limit, and to reduce this on any version of Vista you need to edit the registry.

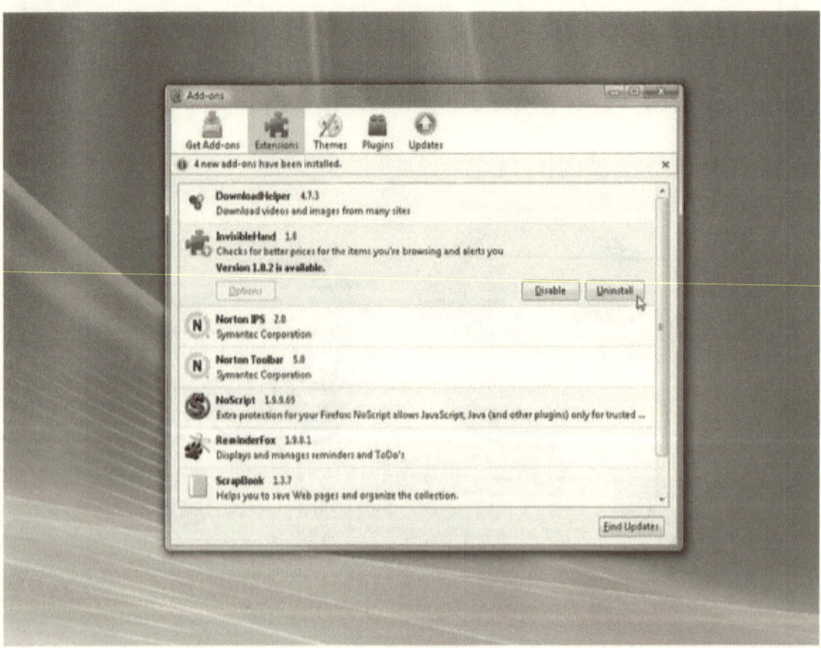

Here's How to Do It:
1. Go to Start and type **"regedit".**
2. In Regedit, navigate to
"HKEY_LOCAL_MACHINE\SOFTWARE\Policies\Microsoft\Windows"
3. Next, right-click on Windows and create a new key called **"Psched",** then right click on the right and create a new "DWORD" entry. Name it **"NonBestEffortLimit"** and set the value to **zero** to disable reserve bandwidth.

Vista Speed Tweak #4 – Modify Your Browser for Optimum Speed

Finally, not only was your Vista operating system not configured by default to blaze the Internet as fast as possible, but neither was your Internet browser! The below instructions show how to increase your browsing speed on Firefox and IE.

Here's How to Do It – Firefox:

1. First, in Firefox type, "*about:config*" into the address bar. *Note:* ignore any warnings displayed.

2. Next, in the filter field, type "*network*" and scroll down to "*network.http.pipelining*" and set it to TRUE, and set "*network.http.pipelining.maxrequests*" from 4 to any number from 8 to 12.

Note: This one change can possibly increase your page-load time by a factor of 30% - 50%.

Here's How to Do It – Internet Explorer:

1. Go to *Start* and type "*regedit.*"

2. Next navigate to "*HKEY_CURRENT_USER\Software\Microsoft\Windows\Current Version\Internet Settings*" and find "*MaxConnectionsPer1_0Server*" and "*MaxConnectionsPerServer.*"

3. Set these to at least 10, or a little higher if you would like. You should also see an increase in performance for IE after making this change as well.

Increase Connection Speed Con't

Vista Speed Tweak #5 – Increase DNS Cache
This is one tweak that PC owners should do anyway, as it can significantly save time while browsing the web, especially if you tend to visit the same sites often. What the DNS cache does is store IP information retrieved from the nameservers so that the next time you visit the same site, your browser doesn't have to waste time retrieving the same information again.
This can be optimized by increasing the size of your DNS cache. This is another registry edit.

Here's How to Do It:
1. Go to *Start* and type *"regedit"* and navigate to *"HKEY_LOCAL_MACHINE\SYSTEM\CurrentControlSet\Servic es\Dnscache\Parameters"*
2. Next right click on the white space at the right and add these four DWORD values: *CacheHashTableBucketSize, CacheHashTableSize, MaxCacheEntryTtlLimit* and *MaxSOACacheEntryTtlLimit*.

3. After checking a list of sites for the optimum setting for these values, the consensus seems to be:
Decimal settings of *CacheHashTableBucketSize* to 1
CacheHashTableSize to 384,
MaxCacheEntryTtlLimit to 64000
MaxSOACacheEntryTtlLimit to 301.
4. Now instead of using those old DNS servers, why not use OpenDNS?
When you're done making all of the changes above, restart your computer and when it boots back up you'll find yourself with a Vista PC that *'burns rubber'* on the Internet!

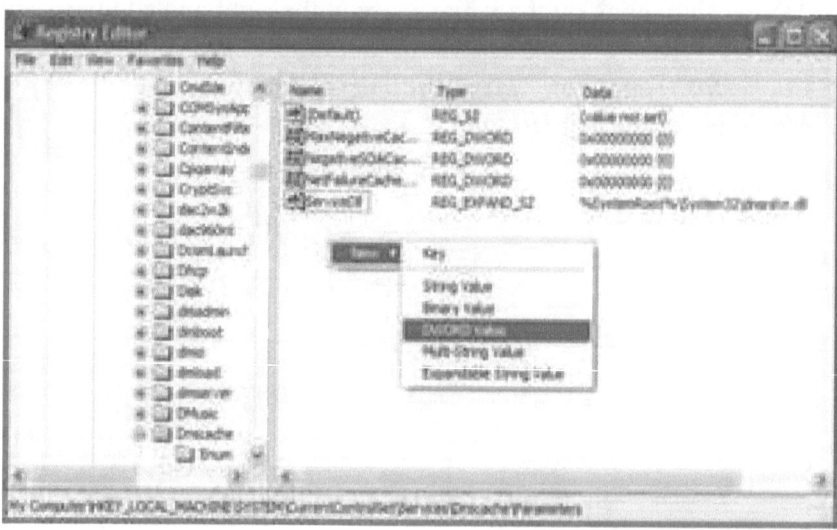

Guide to Speed up Windows 7
Disabling the Search Indexing Feature in Windows 7
The Search Indexing service in Windows 7 will index keeps track of the files so that they can be found quickly when asked at some other time. This feature is useful only if you perform frequent searches on your system.

Here's How to Do It:
1. Right Click the "Computer" Icon in the desktop and select "Manage".
2. Click "Services and Applications" in the "Computer Management" window.
3. Click on "Services". You will see a lot of services listed there. Look for "Windows Search"
4. Right Click on "Windows Search" from the list and choose "Proper-ties".
The "Windows Search Properties Window" will open up.
5. From "Startup type" click on the drop down menu and choose "Disa-bled".
6. Click "Apply" then "OK" and that's it. The Windows 7 Search Indexing Feature is now disabled.

Note: If you want to completely disable the search-indexing feature in Windows 7 you can set the Search Indexing Service to Manual.

Disable the Aero Theme on Windows 7:
If you care more about speed and performance in Windows 7, disabling the Aero theme in Windows 7 certainly will add an extra speed boost to it. Aero user interface squeezes your graphics or video card to its maximum. Disabling the aero theme alone in Windows 7 will really speed things up. You can know this by looking into the memory consumption when aero is turned on and off.

Here's How to Do It:
1. Right Click on your Desktop and select "Personalize" click the Win-dow Color Tab.
2. Uncheck the Box saying "Enable Transparency"
3. Next click on "Open classic appearance properties for more color op-tions". Then a window will open up.
4. Apply a Standard or Basic theme from this window.
5. The Standard Windows 7 theme is more preferred.

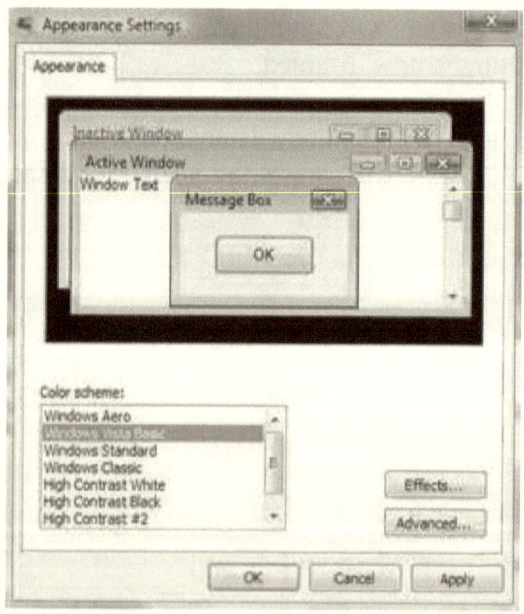

Disabling the Unwanted Visual Effects in Windows 7
Here's How to Do It:
1. First right click on "Computer" and select "Properties".
2. Click on "Advanced System Settings" from the left pane to open up the "System Properties" window.
3. Select the "Advanced" tab from it. Then Under "Performance" click "Settings". Choose the "Custom" options.
4. Next, un-check all the options and select only the last four options (actually only three are needed; you can un tick the second option from the last four).
5. Now just logoff, then log back into your system. You will notice the speed difference now.

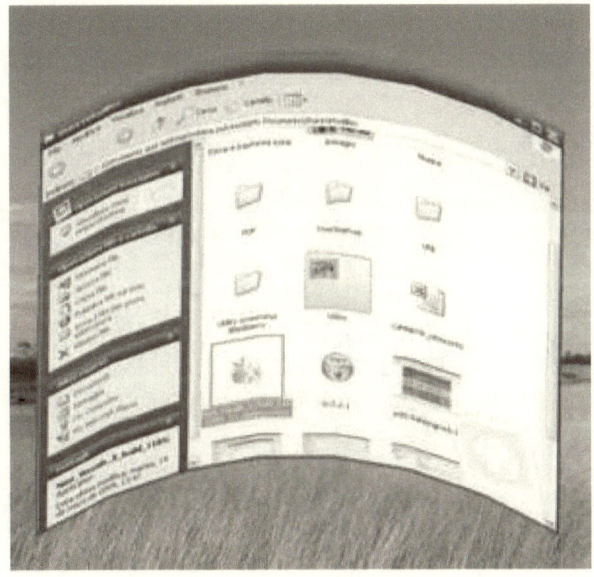

Note: Even though you have tuned off the aero effects in Windows 7 there still are many unwanted visual effects that can be safely disabled to add even more speed to windows 7.

Disabling Unwanted Services to Speed up Windows 7

There are many services in windows 7 that is not require for daily use. For example; some services such as "print spooler" is only needed when you use a printer. If you use a printer only occasionally you can safely turn off that service in Windows 7 and turn it on again only when you need to use a printer. Disabling the unneeded services in Windows 7 can really speed up the system boot time.

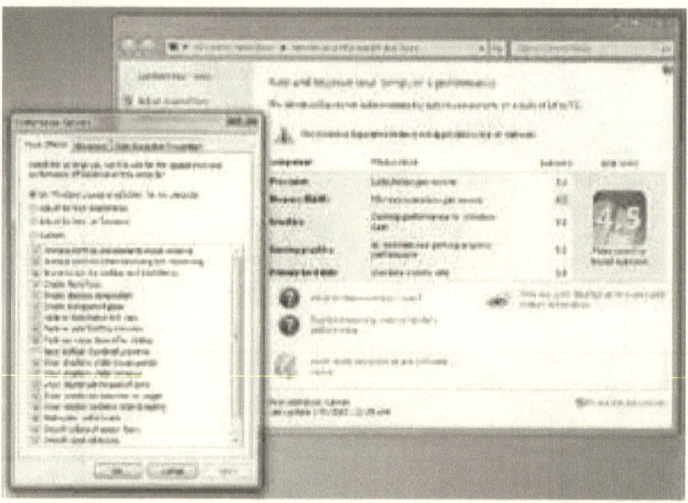

Disable User account control (UAC) Feature in Windows 7
The User account control (UAC) feature in Windows 7 is very annoying though it says it can protect your computer from harmful virus activity etc. But if you are a daily user of your computer this windows 7 feature will be a total nuisance to you. **Note:** Disabling UAC is for advanced users only, it's not recommend doing so if you are not.

Here's How to Do It:
1. From the Control Panel open the " User Accounts and Family Safety " > User Account.
2. Click the User Account Control settings link.
3. Next just Drag the Slider towards "Never Notify".
4. Click "OK" and then reboot your system.

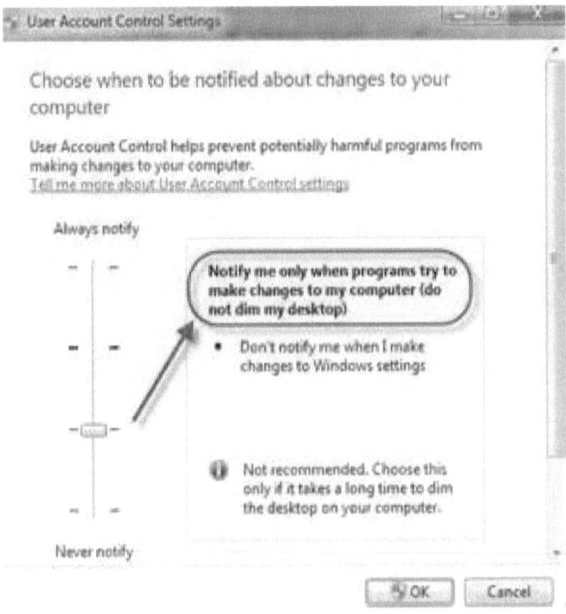

Turn off Unused Windows 7 Features
Here's How to Do It:
1. Open up "Programs and Features" from Control Panel.
2. Click the "Turn Windows features on or off" from the left pane.
3. Next, uncheck all the features that you don't use in Windows 7 and restart the system for the changes to take effect.
Disabling the unused features in Windows 7 that we don't use often will really help in speeding up the system.

Disable the Windows 7 Sidebar Gadgets
Disabling the window 7 sidebar will definitely help you to gain a few se-conds during start up time.
Here's How to Do It:
1. Right click on the sidebar and select "Properties".
2. On the properties windows un-check the box showing "Start sidebar when Windows Starts"
Now windows sidebar won't start when windows 7 start up.

Disable the Aero Peek and Aero Snap features in Windows 7
Here's How to Do It – Aero Snap:

1. In the Windows 7 "Control Panel" and double-click on "Ease of Access Center" icon.
2. Now click on the "Make it easier to focus on tasks " seen at the bottom in there.
3. Now untick the check box saying "Prevent windows from being automatically arranged when moved to the edge of the screen " .
4. Right click on the Windows 7 taskbar and select "Properties ".
5. Now untick the "Use Aero Peek to preview the desktop " option from there.

Aero Snap will help you to maximize, minimize and resize the windows just by dragging and dropping it into the screen corners.

Now To Disable the Aero Peek feature in Windows 7

The Aero Peek feature in Windows 7 helps you to peek through all open windows by hiding all other windows and showing only the outlines of all windows. Aero Peek is similar to the " Show Desktop " Feature in XP and Vista.

If you have followed step 3 then Aero Peek will be automatically disabled. If not, this is how to do it:

Follow these steps to disable Aero Peek:

1. Right-click on the taskbar and select Properties.
2. Then remove the checkmark from "Use Aero Peek to preview the desktop.

You can completely disable Aero Peek on everything, including the taskbar thumbnails by following these steps:

1. Go to Control Panel, then select System Properties.
2. Search for "View advanced system settings"),
3. Next remove the check mark from 'Enable Aero Peek' there.

Change the Power Plan To Maximum Performance

The Power settings in Windows 7 are not automatically set for maximum performance. By default the power plan in Windows 7 is set for a bal-anced performance with energy consumption on hardware. So you may not get the optimal performance from windows 7 if this is the case. So we need to change the power plan to High Performance Mode.

Here's How to Do It:

1. Double click the" Power Options" in the Control panel.
2. Click the down arrow showing" Show Additional Plans" to see the " High Performance " power plan
3. Next, just activate the" High Performance" plan and that's it. You may go for the advanced settings for further tweaking if you like.

Disable the Thumbnail Preview Feature to speed up File browsing in Windows 7

The thumbnail preview feature in Windows 7 will show the small thumbnails of the contents of a folder instead of showing its icon. But this fea-ture really does take up some system resources. So by disabling the Thumbnail Preview feature in Windows 7 the file browsing in Windows 7 can be speed up.

Here's How to Do It:
1. Double Click on 'Computer'
2. Next click on the "Organize" drop-down menu and select the "Folder and Search options"
3. Under 'Files and Folders' section, go to the "View" tab and tick the check box showing "Always show icons, never thumbnails" check box.

In order to maintain your Windows 7 Performance and keep it up in Top Shape there are some very essential software that can help to Speed Windows 7.

Listed below is some Essential Software you can download and use to speed up Windows 7 system.

NOTE: You need to run these utilities at least once a week. and if you do it regularly your Windows 7 will be in top shape every day.

Wise Registry Cleaner
CCleaner
TCP Optimizer
TeraCopy
Startup Delayer

Registry Tweaks to Speed Up Windows 7

There are numerous registry teaks that can be used to speed up windows 7 even more, far too many to discuss here. Below I have supplied a link to only the safest tweaks that can be applied to your PC. Apart from speeding up windows 7 they will also add some functionality in windows like adding Copy to / Move to in right click context menu to speed up your daily tasks.

Go Here:

http://www.computingunleashed.com/2009/01/registrytweaks-for-speeding-up-windows.html

Turn OFF Windows 7 Screen Saver and Wallpaper
Here's How to Do It"
1. Right click on desktop and choose "Personalize".
2. Click the Screen Saver link
3. From the Screen Saver drop down menu, Set it to "None" and click "Apply" and then "OK".
4. Now click on "Desktop Background" link.
5. From the "Location" drop down menu select "Solid Colors" and pick one color and click "OK".
In order to display the wallpaper and screen saver the system needs some memory. So by disabling those two we can save a few Mega Bytes of memory.

Disable Unwanted System Sounds in Windows 7
If you want some real speed boost, sounds played during the Windows 7 start up, shutdown, Logon, logoff, start navigation etc should be set to none. Though, you can keep some of your favorite sounds turned on if you want.
In order to play the sounds you hear in windows 7, system resources are being utilized. So if you can disable these sound effects you can gain some speed and also free some system resources too. Following these steps will certainly boost the speed and performance of your windows 7 operating system.

Here's How to Do It:
1. Type **mmsys.cpl** in RUN From the Windows 7 Start Menu search box and press [Enter].
2. Navigate to the "Sounds" tab.
3. Now from under "Sound Scheme:" select "No Sounds" > Click " Apply" > "OK".

Windows 8 Users:
Windows 8 by default reserve approximate 20% of your bandwidth for its own use if you are using a broadband connection, all is due to the Windows 8 frequent updates and validation processes, if we will disable this in Windows 8 we can use that rest of 20% internet speed which had been settled for updates.

How to enhance the speed of your broadband connection in Windows 8
1. Click on start menu using Metro UI in Windows 8 by pressing Win-dows key. Now type "gpedit.msc" and Click to open. The window Local Group Policy Editor will open:
2. Next go to the Computer Configuration given at the right pane of the Window than click on Administrative Template then Network, select QOS Packet Scheduler, and here click on Limit Reservable Bandwidth.
   3. In the Window Limit Reservable Bandwidth you will see enabled radio button at the right side and give the Bandwidth limit 0% and then apply, this action will change the default system bandwidth to 0% and it will make 100% bandwidth available for you to use on Windows 8.

***

Note: The current Windows 8 build is quite raw and changing memory related power options can cause system instability. Use any of the memory power management settings mentioned here at your own risk.

Outside factors that affect connection speeds
Unfortunately, there are events and conditions that are outside your control. Even with a fast connection, external factors, such as busy websites or spreading computer viruses, can slow the entire web. Popular websites can become overwhelmed with users. For example, when a television commercial mentions a website, many people might try to visit the site at the same time. If the website isn't prepared to handle the traffic, you might encounter delays.

During times of heavy computer virus outbreaks, the Internet can slow down. Many viruses spread by causing computers to send out hundreds or thousands of copies of the virus. This can slow the Internet by sheer volume.

Local Internet congestion can also result in slower-than-normal connection speeds. These slowdowns occur when many people try to connect to the Internet at the same time, and they occur most often at peak activity times, such as after-school hours when students get home and connect to the web.

If you're on a corporate network, general network and proxy server use can affect your Internet performance. Most network administrators monitor Internet use, and will try to keep people from doing things like down-loading large files during peak hours. If you find that your Internet access is slow at times, you might discuss it with your network administrator.

This is especially true in Laptops and Netbooks where the processor speed is altered in accordance to energy settings (and if you are running on battery power)

Here's How to Do It:

Windows XP built-in Power Options

1. Go to the control panel.

2. Choose the 'Performance and maintenance section', and then select 'Power Options'.

3. Here you have the choice of switching from the default High Performance settings to either Automatic or Battery Saver modes. Be aware that this may affect your machine's performance, so you might have to experiment for a while and see if any trade-off is worthwhile.

Windows Vista Power Options

You no longer need to choose between the Hibernation mode and a total shut-down in Vista: the new Sleep mode combines the benefits of the two. It saves the necessary data about your current work to your disk rather than the computer memory. This means your computer can pretty much stop drawing power while it's in Sleep, but can get you up and working much quicker when you come back to your machine.

Sleep mode is now the default mode when you leave your machine unattended for a fixed time, so think very carefully about changing this setting.

Here's How to Do It:

1. In the Power Options, Control Panel, choose High Performance.

2. Next click 'Change plan settings' button, and set 'Put the computer to sleep to Never'.

3. Then click Save Changes.

Set Computer's Energy Settings to High Performance Con't.

Windows 7: Manage Power Settings

There is new power management options that you can set up in Windows 7 compared to XP. You might want to change plans to save battery power on your laptop, or reduce energy consumption.

1. To access power plan options, type power settings into the search bar in the Start Menu and hit Enter.

2. The Power Options screen opens and from here you can select from three predefined plans–Balanced, Power saver, or High performance.

3. Click on Choose what the power button does and you can tweak several options such as requiring a password on wake up and what the power button on the computer does. If you set when I press the power button to do nothing, you won't have a problem with the PC shutting down when you accidentally hit the power button.

4. To change any one of the predefined power plans click on Change plan settings. Then you can change the amount of inactive time before the monitor is turned off or the computer goes into Sleep mode.

5. If you want to revert back to the default settings, simply click on Re-store default settings for this plan.

Windows 8: Manage Power Settings

Windows 8 brings extra memory power management options to Windows Power Plan Advanced Settings which is accessible from Power Options. These options provide the utility to monitor short memory history, channel power history, back off channel heat break tolerance, back off idle utility threshold, and so on. It can help you specify power management settings for your computer's memory.

1. Go to Power Options from Control Panel or click on the power icon from system tray and select More Power Options. Once done, click Change Plan Settings for a specific power plan.

2. Now click Change Advanced Power settings to configure the new pow-er option features.

3. The new options are located in Memory Power Management section: There will be several available options listed there.

Re-Partition and Re-Format Hard Drive

Although time-intensive, a re-partition and re-format of the hard disk drive, along with a clean installation of Windows XP will improve performance. Performing this task will remove all of your existing data, so a back-up or file copy is recommended first. Only save the files you created, as you will need to reinstall each application on the new installation of Windows. If you did not change the default location when saving documents, it may be safe to copy only the user folder and all files and folders within it (ie: "C:\Documents and Settings\(your user name)").
Typically, most users will need to be sure to copy these files:
1. Documents created using applications such as Microsoft Word or similar office suite programs.
2. Bookmarks/Favorites from your Internet browser.
3. Fonts installed that are not included by default with Windows (note that some fonts are installed by applications).
4. E-mail in-box and folders if you use an e-mail client that does not use an Internet browser.
5. Any schedule data for programs such as Outlook
6. Financial records for programs such as Quicken.

Things to do before you partition and format the hard disk:
1. Determine the type of file system that you want to use
You can use either the NTFS or FAT file systems. NTFS is the preferred file system to format the hard disk unless you want to run an earlier version of Windows that cannot read NTFS partitions
2. If you have updated device drivers for peripheral devices, back them up
If you have installed an updated device driver for your peripheral devices (for example, modems and printers), make sure that you back up the new driver for the device to a location other than the drive that you want to format and partition so that you can reinstall it after you install your oper-ating system.

3. Configure your computer to start from the CD or DVD drive

To start your computer from the Windows XP CD, your computer must be configured to start from the CD or DVD drive. In some cases, you may have to modify your computer's BIOS settings to set this configuration.

How to partition and format the hard disk using the Windows XP Setup program

To use the Windows XP Setup program to partition and format the hard disk. Use these steps:

Here's How to Do It:

Step 1 Partition the hard disk

1: Insert the Windows XP CD into your CD or DVD drive, or insert the first Windows XP Setup disk into the floppy disk drive, and then restart the computer to start the Windows XP Setup program. 2. Follow the Instructions on your Screen.

3. If you are using the Windows XP Setup disks, insert each additional disk when you are prompted, and then press ENTER to continue after you insert each disk.

Note: All existing partitions and non-partitioned spaces are listed for each physical hard disk. Use the ARROW keys to select an existing partition, or create a new partition by selecting the non-partitioned space where you want to create a new partition. You can also press C to create a new partition using non-partitioned space.

If you want to create a partition where one or more partitions already exist – do this:

1. You must first delete the existing partition or partitions, and then create the new partition.

2. You can press D to delete an existing partition, and then press L (or press ENTER, and then press L if it is the System partition) to confirm that you want to delete the partition.

3. Repeat this step for each existing partition that you want to include in the new partition.

4. When all the partitions are deleted, select the remaining non-partitioned space, and then press C to create the new partition.

5. To create the partition with the maximum size, press ENTER. To specify the partition size, type the size in megabytes (MB) for the new partition, and then press ENTER.

6. If you want to create additional partitions, repeat steps g. and h.

7. To format the partition and install Windows XP, go to step 2.

Step 2: Format the hard disk and install Windows XP

1. Use the ARROW keys to select the partition where you want to install Windows XP, and then press ENTER.

2. Select the format option that you want to use to format the partition. You can select from the following options:

Format the partition by using the NTFS file system (Quick)

Format the partition by using the FAT file system (Quick)

Format the partition by using the NTFS file system

Format the partition by using the FAT file system

Leave the current file system intact (no changes).

Press Enter.

After the Windows Setup program formats the partition, follow the instructions that appear on the screen to install Windows XP. After the Windows Setup program is finished and you have restarted the computer, you can use the Disk Management tools in Windows XP to create or for-mat more partitions.

Notes If you deleted and created a new System partition, but you are in-stalling Windows XP on a different partition, you are prompted to select a file system for both the System and Startup partitions.

Windows Vista

Create recovery discs, if you don't already have these available. Many computers are no longer sold with CDs; instead, the recovery discs are copied to a partition on the hard drive, or in some cases you can order new disks from the manufacturer. You should make a set of backup disks at the earliest opportunity so you can reinstall the OS if your PC becomes infected with a virus or suffers a catastrophic system failure.

Here's how to do it

1. Click on the Windows "Start" menu and type "recovery" in the "Start Search" area.

2. Click on "Recovery Disk Creation" in the search results and follow the on-screen prompts. You'll need three blank DVDs or seven CDs to create a set of recovery disks.

NOTE: If you have your Windows Vista installation CD, you can skip this step and go on to the next.

3. Insert the Windows Vista recovery disc in the computer's optical drive.

4. Restart the computer. As the computer reboots, a screen will appear asking whether you want to boot from the hard drive or the CD/DVD. Choose the latter and follow the on-screen prompts.

NOTE: Make sure you opt to reformat the drive and not recover it.

Windows 7:

1. Click "Start," then Control Panel." Type "recovery" into the search box and then press "Enter."

2. Select "Restore Your Computer or Reinstall Windows" from list of op-tions. Click "Advanced Recovery Methods."

3. Choose "Reinstall Windows (Requires Windows Installation Disc)" from the menu. Click "Yes," "Skip," then "Restart" to boot to the Windows 7 DVD.

4. Choose your input method from the drop-down menu and then click "Next." Insert the Windows 7 DVD into the disc drive and click "Yes."

5. Follow the on-screen instructions to reformat the computer and re-install Windows 7 to the hard drive.

Windows 8

Go to the disk management utility by simply going through Start menu –> Control Panel–>Administrative Tools–>Computer Man-agement–>Disk Management. Follow the onscreen instructions when prompted, to format a particular drive.

Performance Monitor

Performance Monitor is a simple yet powerful visualization tool for viewing performance data, both in real time and from log files. With it, you can examine performance data in a graph, histogram, or report.

The Performance Monitor is found in the Task manager, under the Performance tab and provides a graphical display of CPU usage history and physical memory usage history. The CPU usage will vary quite a bit over time, depending upon what the computer is doing.

The physical memory shouldn't vary too much if no applications are running. If you're running applications, the physical memory monitor will show how much available memory is being consumed in real time.

The Performance Monitor also gives you access to the Resource Monitor, which will show you the CPU usage, over the last 60 seconds, the I/O speed for the hard disk, the network utilization and the number of hard faults per second that are recorded by the system. This information can be useful, especially if one application is registering a significant number of faults.

Within the Resource Monitor are tabs that will provide additional information about processes, disk usage, network activity, memory usage and CPU usage. This information can be invaluable when trying to determine the source of a fault, or slow computer performance.

Here's How to Do It:
1. Press the ctrl.>alt.> and delete key at the same time to bring up 'Task Manager'
2. Click on Performance Tab
3. From there you can view your CPU and Page File usage. Also Memory info.

Increase Laptop Battery Life

Laptop Power Management - Laptop computers are extremely convenient, allowing us to connect to the internet from just about anywhere in the world. Though, a battery life of at least a couple hours would be a great benefit, there are ways to manage your laptop's power, and increase it's battery life.

Here's How to Do It:
Laptop power settings in Windows XP:
1. Click **Start** > **Control Panel** > **Performance and Maintenance** > **Power Options**
2. Select the **Max Battery** power scheme from the drop-down menu
3. Change the settings to maximize your laptop's power savings.
4. Set the time that the computer should turn off the monitor and hard disk
5. Choose the settings for **standby** or **hibernation** mode. To save the most battery power, reduce these settings below their default values and click **Apply**
6. Select **Portable/Laptop** from the power scheme drop-down list. Ad-just these settings for times when your laptop will be plugged into a power outlet. For best results, set the display to turn off after only a few minutes of inactivity.
7. Adjust the settings for other power management options so that your laptop will wait at least an hour to turn off the hard drive or go to sleep. This will allow for the best possible system performance for your laptop.
8. Click **Apply**.

Laptop power settings in Windows Vista, 7 and 8:
1. Click **Start** > **Control Panel** > **System and Maintenance** > **Power Options**
2. Click Select a **Power Plan**.
3. Choose **Power Saver** to conserve the most battery power4, Choose **Balanced** or **High Performance** if you plan to plug your laptop into a power outlet
5. Click **Choose when to turn off the display**. In the next window, change the settings for when your laptop's monitor should turn off and select when the computer should go to sleep. For the greatest battery power savings, choose times between five and 15 minutes. For best performance, choose times between 30 minutes and one hour.
6. Then click **Change Advanced Plan Settings** and click the plus sign next to **Battery** to adjust settings for the Power Saver power plan. Choose what you want Vista to do when the battery is low or critical. Hibernate is your best option if you have plenty of hard drive space.
Note: If you choose **Shut Down** from the drop-down menu, make sure you save your work often when your laptop is on battery power.
7. Click **Start** > **Control Panel** > **Mobile PC** and select **Windows Mobility Center** and use the slider to adjust your display's brightness settings. This will conserve power without turning off your monitor entirely. You can also monitor your battery status in Windows Mobility Center.

Chapter 4

More Computer Tips

WIRELESS ROUTER

Check Wireless Router for Conflicts

Make sure your wireless router doesn't conflict with a cordless phone or wireless camera. Wireless routers come in three varieties; 802.11 b, g, and n (2.4Ghz) or 802.11 a (5.8Ghz) If you are using a 2.4Ghz Cordless phone and 2.4Ghz Wireless router then your Internet connection speed will slow while you use the cordless phone. The same is true of wireless security cameras. Check on your phone and camera, if it's 900Mhz then it's fine. If it says 2.4Ghz or 5.8Ghz then it could be the cause of your slow connection speed while they're in use.

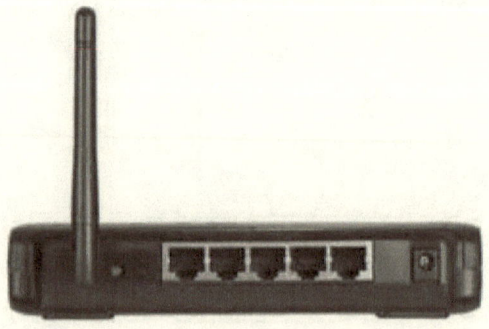

Wireless Router Firmware

Firmware is built-in programmable logic that is contained within most **Wireless routers**. A tested version of firmware provided by the manufacturer is included with every wireless router shipped. This firmware is embedded software that implements network and security protocols for a specific model of hardware device. However, most routers are also designed to support a firmware **upgrade process.** This feature allows the manufacturer to provide enhancements to routers that are already sold.

Note: Manufacturers generally provide firmware upgrades as free downloads from their Web site. A few manufacturers (like Linksys) provide their firmware as open source code on the Internet.
Programmers worldwide can modify and extend the code with new features for their routers.
Note: There are several versions of this **hacked firmware** that can be found on the Web, however, the average homeowner should avoid these types of firmware.

The Firmware Update Process
A firmware upgrade can begin by downloading a binary file package from the manufacturer's Web site. After the package is set up properly on a PC, an administrator can launch the actual upgrade from the wireless router's administrative console.
Note: If the upgrade fails to complete, the router will stop functioning. For this reason, manufacturers generally recommend an 'Ethernet' cable be run from the router to the PC to ensure maximum stability during the update. Consult the router's product documentation for details.

Upgrade Your Wireless Router Firmware Con't.

Immediately after purchasing a router, check the firmware version to ensure it is the latest version. Then, check the manufacturer's Web site occasionally over time for any new firmware upgrade postings. Each time a firmware upgrade is posted, the manufacturer will provide notes detailing the enhancements it provides.

Note: If the new version does not offer any interesting features it would be best to skip an upgrade. However, if a router is performing sluggishly, freezing unexpectedly or experiencing dropped connections, a firmware upgrade often supplies a quick fix.

Check the manufacturer's web site for firmware downloads for your rout-er. Compare this with your version, and upgrade if necessary. Most rout-ers have web interfaces for managing this, check for any labels on your router specifying default address, username and password.

List of wireless router firmware projects
From *Wikipedia, the free encyclopedia*:
The following is a list of firmware modifications for wireless routers that have been created and are maintained by people and groups other than the manufacturer of the product. Most of these originated because vendors were compelled to make their source code public as part of it was based on software licensed under the terms of the GNU General Public License. The Linksys WRT54G series was the starting point for many of these projects.

Third-party firmware projects
Many of these will run on various brands of Linux-based devices, such as Linksys, Asus, Netgear etc. The extent of support for (and testing on) particular hardware varies from project to project.

Major Projects
1. **OpenWrt** - Customizable firmware written from scratch with a combined
2. **SquashFS/JFFS2** file system and the package manager **opkg[1] (Linux/GPL)**
3. **Bluebox** - OpenWrt-based automatic open Internet scanning and bridging software that runs on WRT54G.
4. **Chillispot - Captive portal** software that runs on OpenWrt, available under **GPL.**
5. **FON - Chillispot**-based worldwide Hotspot network. After unsuccessfully attempting to develop a version that supports 2 SSIDs (one private, one public), FON abandoned the WRT54G series, and now distributes a router called La Fonera, which does support 2 SSIDs.
6. **Coova** - OpenWrt based with focus on Wireless Hotspot functionality.
7. **Freifunk** - OpenWrt-based, German software supports wireless mesh networks with **OLSR** and **B.A.T.M.A.N.**
8. **Meraki** - OpenWrt-based Mesh Networking Wifi AP developed through Roofnet project
9. **OpennetFirmware** - Firmware based on OpenWrt and parts of Freifunk.

10. **PacketProtector** - OpenWrt-based security distribution that includes IDS, IPS, VPN, and web antivirus capabilities.

11. **Gargoyle** - A web interface for OpenWrt that places a strong emphasis on usability. Features include an AJAX interface, dynamic DNS, QoS, bandwidth monitoring and access restrictions. **(Linux/GPL)**

12. **LuCI** - A web interface for OpenWrt written in **Lua**

13. **X-Wrt** - A web interface for OpenWrt[3] (Linux/GPL)

14. **UseMyNet** - Captive Portal and Hotspot software that runs on OpenWrt.

15. **WiFiDog Captive Portal** - WiFi Dog by **Ile Sans Fil,** a Captive Portal software that runs on the OpenWrt platform.

16. **WifiTastic** - Hotspot solution for home or small business use. Features credit card billing. Runs on the OpenWrt platform.

17. **Wirds.net** - A project which uses **freifunk** firmware with **chillispot** captive portal and worldspot.net authentication.

18. **HotSpotPA** - Captive portal hotspot system with credit card billing, based on OpenWrt.[5]

19. **DD-WRT** - Based on OpenWrt code. Paid and free versions available. **(Linux/GPL)**

Note: AutoAP - AutoAP is an add on to DD-WRT that allows routers to continuously scan for and connect to open (and predefined WEP) wireless networks.

19. **Tomato - HyperWRT**-based firmware. Features advanced QoS as well as **Ajax** and 20. **SVG** graphs. The **Tomato Manual** is available at Wikibooks. **(Linux/GPL)**

21. **DebWRT** - Debian on embedded devices (Combines the Linux kernel from

22. **OpenWrt** and the **package management system** from **Debian (Linux/GPL)**

23. **Sveasoft** - Paid and free versions available. Latest versions available via subscription.

34. **RouterTech**.Org - The RouterTech firmware supports a vast number of ADSL Modem/Routers based on the **Texas Instruments AR7** chipset, with either the **Adam2** or **PSP** boot loaders. The firmware supports wireless routers using the **TNETW1130** and **TNETW1350A** wifi chips, and also non-wireless routers. Features include support for **minix** partitions, **CIFS** and ftpfs mountpoints, selectable DSP and tiatm drivers, the latest 35. **Busybox** releases, udpxy, dnsproxy, siproxd, mjproxy, ad blocking, **scp,** miniupnp, netshaper, rshaper, among others. **(Linux/GPL)**

Minor Projects
1. **BatBox** - RAM based distribution for experimenting, does not change firmware.
2. **Earthlink's IPv6** Firmware - IPv6 feature added to original Linksys firmware (beta-test version).
3. **EzPlanet** - Enhanced firmware based on DD-WRT v24 and including Layer 2 Load Balancer.
4. **Neighbornode**

5. **Tarifa** - Based on stock WRT54GL firmware.

6. **TinyPEAP** - Secure wireless authentication feature added to Linksys firmware.

7. **WiFi-Box** - No documentation available as of January 2006.

8. **OpenWAG200** - A firmware based on stock firmware for the Linksys WAG200G modem/routers.

Not maintained Projects

1. **EWRT** - Enhanced WRT, with integrated captive portal based on NoCatSplash

2. **FreeWRT** - Experimental firmware based on OpenWrt.

3. **HyperWRT** - Original power boost firmware project by Avenger 2.0 to stay close to official WRT54G and WRT54GS firmware but add features such as transmit power, port triggers, scripts, telnet, etc.

4. **HyperWRT** +tofu — Based on stock WRT54GS firmware, HyperWRT and some additions.

5. **Rupan HyperWRT** - Based on stock WRT54G firmware and HyperWRT.

6. **HyperWRT** Thibor - Firmware based on stock WRT54GS firmware, HyperWRT (closed) +tofu and other additions.

Note: Upgrading your router firmware, upgrading your router/firewall equipment, replacing your old cable modem, and downloading **Google Web Accelerator** will help to improve your Internet connections.

If you have multiple computers sharing a connection, make sure all the computers are physically connected to a router or switch, and not just to a hub. Hubs are **"dumb"**, low-level equipment, while **routers** are capable of prioritizing and directing traffic effectively.

How to Set Up a Home Network
1. Turn off the computer and install the manufacturer's adapter. **Note:** If you're putting a PCI card into a desktop computer, you'll have to open the case to do so.
2. Plug the adapter into a phone jack. If a telephone or fax machine is already using the jack, plug the phone or fax into the adapter first. If you're short on phone jacks, you may want to use a two-way splitter to share the jack.
3. Turn the computer on. Windows will detect the adapter and prompt you to install the driver from the included CD-ROM.
4. Follow the on-screen instructions. Depending on the package you're using, you might also be prompted for the computer's name.
5. Restart the computer.
6. If you plan to share an Internet connection and don't have a router, install the Internet-sharing software (if included by the manufacturer).

Home Network

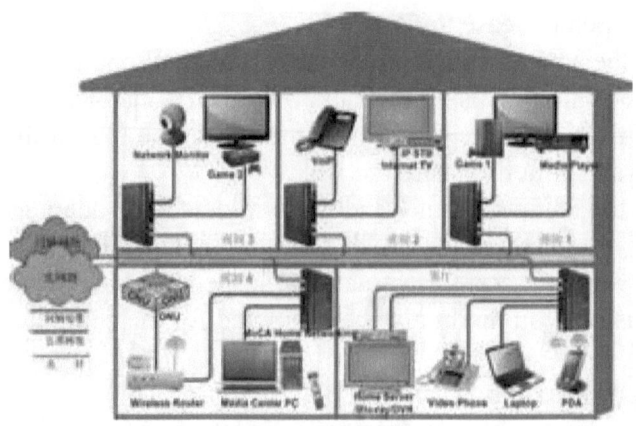

Reset Your Home Network

You might experience network or Internet connection issues in Windows for a number of reasons. Some common issues that can cause these problems are:
1. A wireless network adapter switch that's not enabled
2. WEP, WPA, or WPA2 security key or passphrase issues
3. Cables that aren't connected properly
4. Corrupted or incompatible drivers
5. Missing updates
6. Network connection settings
7. Hardware or software problems
Sometimes restarting (or unplugging and replugging the electric power on) your home network or your router (if you have one) will drastically increase the speed of your connection.
How to Trouble Shoot Your Network
If you are having problems with your home network, follow the steps below to help isolate and troubleshoot the configuration of your home network's basic connectivity, and file and printer sharing.

Here's How to Do It:
Windows XP:
First, try to isolate and resolve the issue by using the steps in the Windows XP Home and Small Office Networking Troubleshooter in Help and Support Center.
1. Click **Start**, and then click **Help and Support**.
2. Under **Pick a Help Topic**, click **Networking and the Web**.
3. Under **Networking and the Web**, click **Fixing networking or Web problems**, and then click **Home and Small Office Networking Troubleshooter**.
4. Answer the questions in the troubleshooter to try to find a solution.

Note: You may need to know the kind of network structure that you are using to complete these steps. If you are not sure, go to the "Home-network structures and their configurations" section.

Windows Vista, Windows 7 and 8:
Vista comes with a set of new network diagnostics tool built in. Vista is perhaps the most relevant in quickly establishing the connectivity status is the Network Connectivity Status Indicator (NCSI).

Also fundamentally different in the **Windows Vista** and **Windows 7** internals is the networking and internet control software. Microsoft introduced several new components to Windows Vista networking with the intention of improving performance. However, these changes had a detrimental effect on network performance for some users.

If you cannot connect to the internet at all on a **Windows Vista** or **Windows 7** machine, you may wish to try the network troubleshooter. You can also try a **'Winsock reset',** which resets all of Windows core net-working components.

If you are having problems with internet or network speed in **Windows Vista** or **Windows 7,** you may wish to run the Internet **Connectivity Evaluation Tool** to check that your home networking equipment is up to spec.

There are also several networking settings you can tweak in *Windows Vista* and **Windows 7.**

Windows 7
1. First, launch the **Network and Internet Troubleshooter**. This is done via the **Network and Sharing Center** from the control panel.
2. To launch the control panel, select the Windows 7 Orb and select the Control Panel option as shown below:
3. By default, the control panel window is organized by category. Select **View network status and tasks** to reach the **Network and Sharing Center**.
4. Once in the **Network and Sharing Center** there is an option at the bottom of the window to **troubleshoot problems**, select this option and the **Network and Internet troubleshooting** window will open.
5. Answer the Questions in the Troubleshooter to try and find a Solution.

Replace Your Old Cable Modem

A DSL modem is like any other piece of networking equipment - if operated in a proper environment (well ventilated with no temperature extremes, and kept free of dust), it should easily last years, but because of the possibility that any solid state electronics device will degrade over time due to accumulated heat damage, you very well could be missing out on some connection speed by using an older modem. Your broadband modem will have a harder and harder time 'concentrating' on maintaining a good connection as it gets older (signal to noise ratios will go down, and the number of resend requests for the same packet will go up).

The newer modems are probably going to have a higher signal to noise ratio tolerance. Meaning they will work when noise gets into the line. The newer modems will probably have better reporting tools built into the modem - like a built in signal to noise ratio meter and signal strength meter. Keep in mind, that no matter how fast or snazzy a new modem might be, it's still only going to transfer data as fast as your line is configured for. Consequently, the only time you'll want an upgrade or replacement is if your modem fails, or if your ISP says you do. That may happen if the ISP changes characteristics of your line, including, perhaps, the speed or underlying technology.
Note: An after-market cable modem as opposed to a cable-company modem has been known to offer a better connection. Check with your Internet Service Provider to see if there is an upgrade for your old modem.

Router/Firewall Equipment

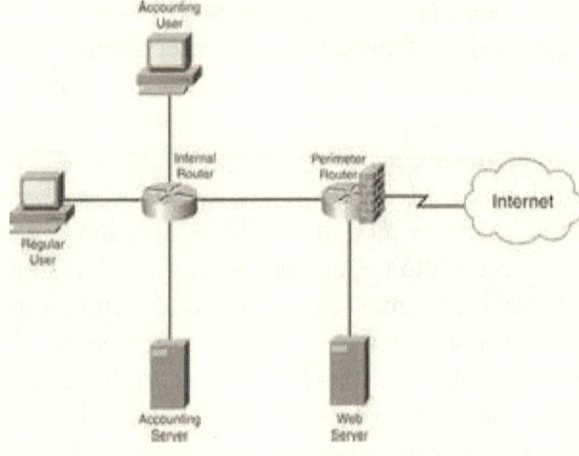

Upgrade Your Router/Firewall Equipment

Maybe it's time to upgrade your old router/firewall equipment.
Today, nearly everyone is using the Internet for a variety of reasons, and many of us require quick and easy access, particularly for business tasks. *Fiber Optic Internet, DSL*, and *ADSL* are some of the methods that can be used to connect to the internet.

Fiber optics is the fastest method of accessing the internet, by using a signal that transmits data produced by a computer, at speeds that are much faster than other forms of current internet communication.

Copper and **fiber** transmissions are transforming the Internet, and in many places around the world, these Internet access methods are increasingly replacing older Internet access methods. Today, it is now possible for Internet users to connect using fiber optic Internet access in their offices and homes. Many companies as well, are now offering fiber optic and wireless Internet services to their customers. You can search online to compare the services and prices of the numerous companies that are offering these services.
Specifically, when upgrading your equipment, look into any *speed specifications* (many older routers are not capable of transmitting to/from the in-ternet faster than 10 Mbps, even though the local ports transmit in 100 Mbps). Also, older routers may be under powered, so that even though the theoretical speed is 10 Mbps, the processor on the router is too weak to reach maximum speed.

IMPORTANT NOTE: It is critical that you take steps to protect your wireless connection. For instance, if you are running your own wireless hub/router, it is often possible for *"unwanted guests"* to sneak into your network, (either accidentally or deliberately) through your Internet connection, as well as have full access to your private network.

For this reason, many small networks (and home private networks) use NAT to remap their home or office machines through a DSL (or DSL/Wireless) modem to the Internet. *"NAT"* stands for **"Network Address Upgrade Translation",** which is used to "map" the private IP addresses of individual computers on a local network, to a single IP address (the "NAT's address") on the Internet. A NAT firewall, router or gateway is simply a piece of equipment or soft-ware that makes the bridge between your local network and the Internet, and makes all of the connections appear to be from the NAT address, not the local address of the LAN computer. Also a PAT firewall, router or gateway is effectively the same thing, except that it maps network ports, in addition to IP addresses. For the purposes of the CBL, a PAT is the same as a NAT.

Home PC Firewall Choices
Choices -- Your choices include using the firewall built into Windows, using a third party product, choosing an Internet security suite that in-cludes a firewall, and/or using a hardware firewall router or gateway.
Microsoft Windows Firewall -- The Windows 7, Vista and XP Service Pack 2/3 operating systems have firewalls built in that are turned on by default to block threats from the Internet. You should leave this feature turned on until you replace it with third-party software and/or hardware.

Two-Way Third-Party Personal Firewall Software -- These firewalls block both incoming and outgoing threats. A computer may have outgoing threats when it becomes infected with a virus, Trojan horse or spyware. A challenge for this type of firewall is to distinguish between threats and legitimate software. Three common ways to address this are by vendors including a list of safe software for the firewall to check [white list], malware to block [black list] and/or by issuing a pop up alert to the user ask-ing for advice on what to do [better for experts].

Check to see if Faster Internet Connections are in Your Area

There may be faster internet connections in your area.
As stated in the previous sub-chapter, Fiber Optic and Cable Internet tend to be faster than DSL and Dial-Up.
To determine how fast your Internet is now, you can download one of the various free 'Internet Connection Speed Test' software from the Internet, and follow their instructions, to test your connection speed.
Note: Millions of people are using the Internet at the same time, therefore, each time you test your Internet speed, you can expect to get a different result.
If you are looking to find a faster Internet Service, do a Google search. There are several to choose from online.
For example:
1. FiOS: Fastest Landline Service
Verizon offers the fastest download speeds on the Internet with its FiOS service, which is available in 12 states along the East Coast and in Washington, D.C. FiOS regularly hits download speeds in excess of 35 mega-bits per second, or about 4.5MB of file downloads per second. The draw-back to FiOS is the limited number of places where Verizon has run fiber to the home.
2. 4G LTE: Fastest Wireless Service
The next fastest Internet connection to be had in the U.S. is a 4G cellular data plan. However, 4G has become something of a meaningless term in the U.S. There were three competing standards; one of them -- Sprint's WiMax -- is slowly being retired, and the major carriers appear to be standardizing on LTE connections. The fastest providers tend to vary by region and by the number of users on the network at any given time. Depending on the carrier, your average download speeds on a 4G network can be anywhere from 2 to 4 megabits per second or less for some of the smaller networks, up to 25 or 30 megabits per second. For the two largest carriers, Verizon and AT&T, PC Magazine rates the average download speed at around 11 to 12 megabits per second.

Check to see if Faster Internet Connections are in Your Area
Con't.

Wild Blue high speed internet satellite providers offer high speed internet access over satellite to virtually everywhere in the U.S, and provides much higher speeds than dial up. Wild Blue internet access will surf up to 30 times faster than dial up.

Earthlink Satalite professes to be a super-fast, always-on Internet connection via 2-way satellite that won't tie up your phone. Satellite Internet is available nationwide.

ATT Uverse, Qwest, and **Verizon** are other good services to consider.

Price and Data Caps
Beyond available coverage areas, the other aspect that drives Internet connections is price. FiOS gets expensive as a fixed rate monthly service; it can be triple or quadruple the cost of a comparable cable Internet package on its own. Many service providers bundle services, in part to avoid spending more money in infrastructure. Cable Internet providers may not be as fast as FiOS, but they can combine telephone services, cable TV and cable Internet into one bill.

From their perspective, it all uses the same cable connection; the companies just get to charge more. Bundle deals also happen with wireless data plans, but they're less common. Wireless data plans are also likelier to cost more for greater bandwidth consumption; the benefit, of course, is that your Internet connection isn't tied to your home and can go with you anywhere you have wireless coverage.

Tips to Boost the Speed of Your Internet Connection Right Now!

Note: These Tips Recommended for **'Advanced Users"**
Change Local Area Network (LAN) Settings
1. Start Internet Explorer.
2. Click on "Tools," then "Internet Options,"
3. Then select the "Connections" tab and click the "LAN settings" button.
4. If you see any check marks in any of the options listed, uncheck them.
5. Ensure everything is this window is NOT selected, as shown in the example below, then click Ok.
Rebuild your Winsock – Windows uses something called **"Windows Sockets"** or **"Winsock"** to control the input and the output of data through a network connection. **Winsock**, is a technical specification that defines how Windows network software should access network services, especially TCP/IP. Windows Dynamic Link Library (DLL) also called winsock.dll implements the API and coordinates Windows programs and TCP/IP connections. But sometimes Windows Sockets or Winsock may get corrupted as a result of which you may not be able to connect to the Internet. It may therefore need to be repaired.
The Winsock can often become clogged with **Spyware** and other miscellaneous software knowingly and/or unknowingly acquired through every day "normal" Internet usage. Regardless of the condition of your Winsock, you can safely reset it (whether you need to or not), using the free Winsock rebuilding utility.
NOTE: You will need to re-boot your PC immediately after running this application, so please be sure to save all of your work and close any running programs before you begin this procedure.
Reset Winsock: Windows XP
Here's How to Do It
1. Click Windows Start, then click Run.
2. In the Open: field type CMD, then click OK. The Windows Command Console (**black DOS window**) will appear.
3. At the blinking cursor, type netsh int ip reset c:\Reset.txt
4. Press Enter on the keyboard.

5. At the blinking cursor, type: netsh winsock reset
6. Press Enter.
7. At the blinking cursor, type: exit. This closes the Windows Command Console window.
8. Restart your computer. That's it; you have successfully reset your Winsock.

For those who like to use the click and fix solution, you can down-load a free Winsock XP Fix utility from the Internet.

TweakTester – By default, Windows XP sets something called the "Receive Window" (sometimes referred to as RWIN) to a value much too low for today's modern high-speed Internet demands. By changing this low default value to a specific larger number, your Internet performance should improve. To determine what value your Receive Window should be, you can use one of the free Tweak Tester utilities from the Internet, and follow their instructions.

Reset Winsock: Windows Vista
Here's How to Do It:
1. Click the Windows Start button.
2. Type Cmd in the Start Search text box and press Ctrl-Shift-Enter (key-board shortcut to run Command Prompt as Administrator). Click Con-tinue to allow elevation request.
3. Type netsh winsock reset in the Command Prompt shell, and then press the Enter key.
4. Type netsh int ipv4 reset in the Command Prompt shell, and then press the Enter key.
5. If you use ipv6, type netsh int ipv6 reset in the Command Prompt shell, and then press the Enter key.

Note: you may need to run Network Diagnostics afterwards to "repair" your connection after this.

Reset Winsock: Windows 7
Here's How to Do It:
1. Open CMD as admin, type **netsh winsock reset** and hit Enter.
2. If you are using **IPv4**, type **netsh int ipv4 reset** and hit Enter.
3. If you use **ipv6,** type **netsh int ipv6 reset** and hit Enter.
4. You will have to restart your computer.

Tips to Boost the Speed of Your Internet Connection Right Now! Con't

___

If you'd like to generate a log file of the changes, append a logfile path to the above command, eg. netsh winsock reset c:\winsocklog.txt.

Remember to create a system restore point first.

NOTE: Microsoft **Windows 8** and **Windows Server 2012** introduce new Windows Sockets programming elements. A set of high-speed networking extensions are available for increased networking performance with lower latency and jitter. You can research the internet to read more about this.

Reset Winsock: Windows 8

Windows 8 has a built-in administrator tool, Network Shell (Netsh) that allows you to configure and monitor network adapters on your Windows 8 computer. Netsh can completely reset your network adapter back to its default state. It can also reset the Windows Firewall in Windows 8 too. All you need is a Command Prompt with administrator privileges. After high internet usage, you can run "netsh winsock reset catalog" on your Windows 8 computer.

From an Administrator command prompt, you can type **netsh int ip re-set reset.log** to force your network stack back to the default configuration.To use Netsh, you will need to open a Command Prompt with administrator privileges.

Here are three ways to do this:

Using a mouse

1. Go to the Start menu.
2. Right click the Start menu background to bring up the app commands.
3. Select 'All apps'.
4. Right click 'Command Prompt' tile to bring up the app commands.
5. Select 'Run as administrator'. If you're prompted for an administrator password or confirmation, type the password or provide confirmation. 142

Using a keyboard

1. Go to the Start menu
2. Press the Windows logo key + Z to open the app commands.

3. Press Enter to select 'All apps'.
4. Use the arrow keys to navigate to the 'Command Prompt' tile.
5. Press the Application key to bring up the app commands.
6. Use the arrow keys to navigate to 'Run as administrator' and press Enter. If you're prompted for an administrator password or confirmation, type the password or provide confirmation.

Using touch
1. Go to the Start menu.
2. Swipe up from the bottom of the Start menu to bring up the app commands.
3. Select 'All apps'.
4. Scroll to the 'Command Prompt' tile and press and hold it to bring up the app commands.
5. Select 'Run as administrator'. If you're prompted for an administrator password or confirmation, type the password or provide confirmation.

Google's free Web-Accelerator puts the pedal to the metal! By now you've probably seen many self-proclaimed Internet speed-boosters advertised for *dial-up* users. **So a lot of people with high-speed Internet access have never considered the potential usefulness of a Web-accelerator.** Sure, your Web pages load fast now, but they can load even faster if you **install Google's free Web-Accelerator**. Google uses a number of ingenious strategies to get the Web pages you desire on your desktop very quickly. **Note:** After you install the Google Web-Accelerator, the speed testing sites will not run until you disable it for accurate results.

Steps to temporarily disable the Google Web-Accelerator:
1. Right-click its icon in your system tray (located by the clock in the lower-right corner of your desktop).
2. Next click "Stop Google Web Accelerator.")
3. It will start again automatically when you restart your PC, or you can start it up manually as you would any other program found under your Start Menu.

Contact Your Internet Service Provider

Sometimes you may just have bad service. If you contact your Internet service provider (ISP), they can usually tell if your connection is substand-ard without having a technician come to your home. Just give them a call and ask.

If you have a bill or contract agreement available from your cable provider, **see what Internet speed you are paying for.** There should be a reported upload speed (the maximum speed of how fast you can send data) and a reported download speed (the maximum speed of how fast you can receive data.) If you cannot find this information, you can always contact your ISP, or Cable Company's technical support, via telephone or email, and ask for this information. Mostly, you are interested in the **download speed,** as most consumers use their Internet connections to *receive* much more information then they will ever send.

If your computer is slow, or starting to show its age, it may be time for an upgrade. No matter how fast your Internet connection is, the whole thing will just seem slow if you can only access the Internet as fast as your PC will allow you to do so.

Be realistic. The "high end" computer purchased as new 5 years ago *may* run the latest version of Windows, but that doesn't mean that it will do it very well. Technology marches on and it seems there is a game of "one-up-man-ship" played between software developers and hardware design-ers. Regardless, eventually new software will require new hardware or vice versa. It seems that the amount of frustration you can endure best determines how long you will run your current setup.

Note: Adding RAM is often the most cost-effective *upgrade* you can make to speed up a sluggish computer. As opposed to *upgrading* your processor which would most likely cost as much as buying a new computer.

Upgrade the Hard Drive
Maybe it's time to consider replacing the computer's internal drive . Even if your present drive has plenty of unused capacity, hard drives are fragile beasts that often go bad after two or three years. A newer drive will often read and write data faster, thus improving your machine's performance.

HARD DRIVE

Replace Your Old Monitor
Consider investing in a new monitor instead of upgrading your computer. If you're still using an old-fashioned, boxed shape monitor, it limits your ability to work with more than one program at a time. A flat-panel monitor with a wide screen format is ideal for viewing DVDs or movie downloads, and when it's time to work.

Even though an older computer can run several programs at once, with a wide screen monitor, you can easily keep two or three programs constantly in view. Now you're more productive, even if your old computer's no more powerful than before.

Replace Your Old Key Board and Mouse
In some cases a new keyboard, and mouse is probably a wiser purchase than a new computer. (ie; keys missing, sticking or not working. Mouse sluggish or hangs).

Replace Your Old PC
The average desktop PC has a functional lifespan of roughly *two* to *five* years, depending upon the type of system purchased, advances in hard-ware components and changes in the software running on it.

Note: A desktop computer has a better advantage over a laptop because a greater amount of upgrades can be made to a desktop compared to a laptop computer.

Don't Hold Down a Key too Long

There are only **3 keys** you should hold down on the keyboard.
They Are:

The **Ctrl key, the Shift Key,** and the **Alt key**. The rest you are
supposed to tap quickly or they will repeat themselves. When you
need to use either the **Ctrl, Shift** or **Alt key** in combination with
another key, hold down the key first and then tap the other. For
example, a hotkey combination to close an application is Alt +
F4. You would hold down the Alt key while taping F4 to make
this work.

Also, when cleaning a computer's keyboard, be careful not to
press on the keys too long. Use a microfiber cloth and an air
duster to lightly clean any debris from between the keys.

A LOOK INSIDE THE DESKTOP COMPUTER

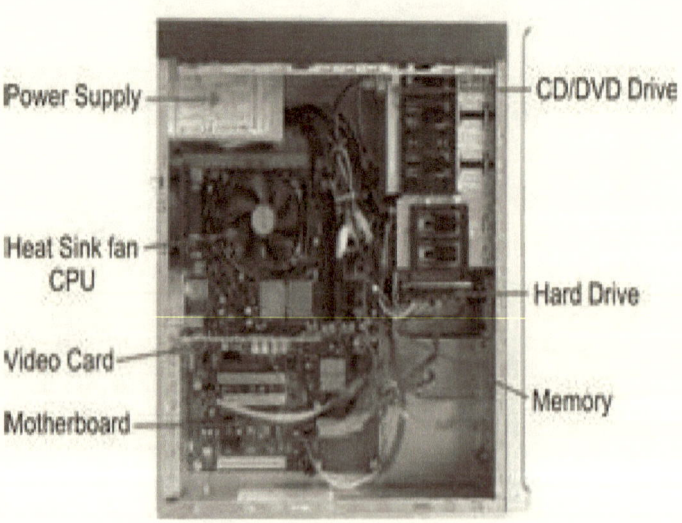

Power Supply

CD/DVD Drive

Heat Sink fan
CPU

Hard Drive

Video Card

Memory

Motherboard

Clean your Computer's Inside

Computer fans pull a lot of dust inside the chassis. If undisturbed, the dust can interfere with ventilation, eventually causing parts to fail. Dust blocking the fans and heat sink inside the computer can cause performance problems, including memory problems.

First dust off the fans, then clean the Inside of the Computer. Here's How to Do It:
1 Check your owner's manual to see if the manufacturer has provided specific instructions. If so, follow them.
2 Supplies you might need: A can of compressed air, Spray Electronics cleaner, a soft brush (such as a paintbrush) and an anti-static rag, plus a dust mask if you're allergic to dust.
3 Shut down the computer, and unplug the power cord..
4 Remove the computer cover (see your owner's manual for instructions).

Important Note: Before opening the cover, be sure to ground yourself to the computer's case with an **anti-static grounding strap**. *(You can purchase one at any computer or electronics store)*. Otherwise, you can ground yourself by touching a metal part of the chassis.

5 Once inside, spray compressed air on the fan blades, power supply chassis, drive chassis and circuit boards to remove loose particles and dust.
6 Gently brush off dust and particles that the forced air didn't dislodge.
7 Brush any remaining dust out from the bottom of the chassis.
8 Spray Electronics cleaner onto an anti-static rag, and wipe the inside and outside of the cover thoroughly.
9 Replace the cover and reconnect any hardware you may have disconnected to remove the cover.

Ask a Pro

Seek Help When You Don't Know What You're Doing!

If you don't feel comfortable doing it yourself, call your friendly computer geek for advice, or visit online forums to get help. Moreover the Internet is probably the greatest resource for new information and help when you need it.

Also, check out the help file of the particular user manual for your computer. Make time to read it, and learn what you need to know. You will save a lot of money and time over the long run when you do. Some folks never have time to study what they need to know, but they always seem to have plenty of time to have problems and agonize over them when they happen.

Below I have listed a couple free online support sites: Most of the sites in this category were in operation at the time this book was printed. They have volunteer staffing and that means the quality of answers to your questions can vary widely. At any rate, you can also Google: Online Computer Tech Support or something like that to get professional help.
Tech Support Guy
http://www.techguy.org/
5 Star Support
http://www.5starsupport.com/
Protonic
http://www.protonic.com/

Computer Troubleshooting Flowchart

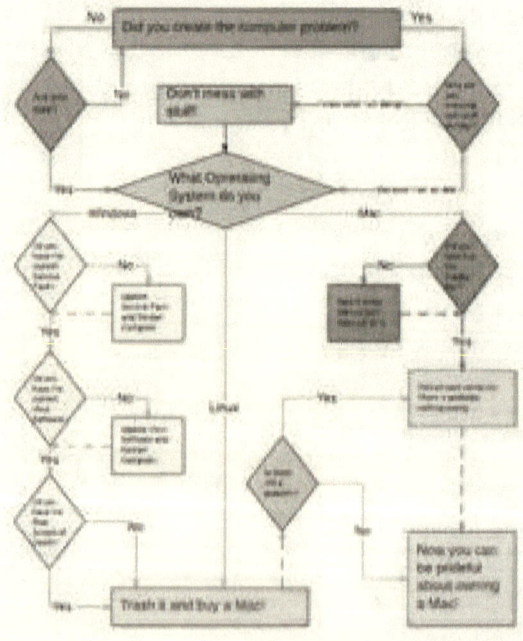

Chapter 5

Basic Troubleshooting and Repair Tips

LED

Power button

What to Do When Your Computer Won't Start

You press the power button on your computer and nothing happens… No lights, no beeps, no fan noise. What is the first thing you do? I don't think there are any computer problems more frustrating than when your computer won't start.

Here's What to Do:

1. First be sure the computer is plugged in! Even if you're absolutely certain that it is connected, double check it.
2. Assuming that it is plugged in, your home's circuit breakers are not tripped, and the power cord is plugged into the back of the computer, you may have a bad power supply.
3. Before you open the computer, look on the back and make sure that the reset button is not tripped. Also look to see that the power supply is set to the correct voltage.
4. To check the power supply, **unplug the power cord**, then open the computer and find the metal box located inside, at the top and back of the computer. **Four screws usually hold it in and the power cable connects to it.** It contains a fan that blows air out the back. Also there will be a wiring harness, with numerous power connectors that are attached to the ends of the wires. These plug into drives, fans, and possibly other components. The harness also will have connectors to the motherboard.
5. When you open the computer, all this wiring can be very intimidating, so study it, and you'll find it less mysterious. Note the connections in writing, and label the wires if necessary.
6. Disconnect the wires and remove the power supply. Take it to the computer store and get a replacement with the same wattage.

The computer comes on, but nothing appears on your monitor.
In other words, Windows never shows up. You may have a **monitor** problem.

Here's What to Do:
1. Try using another monitor that you know is good, on the computer, and see if anything shows up on the screen.
2. If this second monitor works, the first one is bad.

Important Note: Never open the back of a monitor to fix it. The capacitors inside monitors store electricity, and you could be **injured** or even **killed** if you touch one.
Monitors are not worth repairing. **Just buy a new one.**

If the screen is still dark, it could be a video card problem. Here's What to Do:
1. First, find the video card. This is a circuit board that fits into a slot in the motherboard.
2. The cable from the monitor connects to the VGA (video graphics adapter) port, which sticks out through the back of the computer.
3. If the VGA port is part of the motherboard, the video is built in. You can't fix that. Otherwise, it will be part of the video card.
4. Assuming you have a separate card, be sure it is firmly seated. The front end of the card can rise out of the slot inadvertently when the back end is screwed down to the computer frame.
5. If you have a computer that is working perfectly, turn it off and remove the video card. Put the card that works in the problem computer.
6. If the system works, you need a new card. If you don't have an extra card to test your system, you can buy a cheap one. If it doesn't solve the problem, take it back.

```
Loading Operating System ...
Boot from CD/DVD :
Press any key to boot from CD.._
```

If you boot up, and the computer cannot find the C: drive, you might have a bad hard drive.

Here's What to Do:
1. Try rebooting the system. Sometimes, a reboot will work
2. If you have another working computer, swap hard drives to diagnose the problem.
3. If your computer boots with the other hard drive, yours is probably bad..
4. If your drive has enough life to spin up occasionally, transfer your data to another drive, asap.
5. If the drive is dead and you don't have a backup, a computer shop may be able to save your data.

NOTE: Always backup your important data regularly to a flash drive. This will save you in case of hard-drive failure.
Geek Tip: You can seal a nonworking drive in a bag and put it in a freezer overnight. That could shrink things enough to free them up. I've used this trick a few times and it's worth a try.

Steps to Replacing Your Hard Drive:
1. Unplug the *Power Cord,* and open the machine.
2. Protect your mother board from static! Make sure you are grounded by touching the metal casing of the computer.
3. Your hard drive is located inside the computer, in the front of your machine. It will be about the size of a small paperback book and is probably held in by four screws, two on each side. *Power and ribbon cables connect to the back.*
4. Next, Put the new drive in and install it as the master. Reconfigure the old drive as the slave. The instructions that come with the new drive should explain that.

5. Boot the computer and install Windows on the new drive. If you're lucky, the computer will see the old drive (it will be D:). You can then transfer your data to the new drive.
6 You can now, carefully disconnect, and remove the old hard drive, *noting where all the connections go.*

Replacing a hard drive is somewhat more difficult than the other operations. However, changing the hard drive yourself may be worthwhile. Because if you pay to have the work done, it may not be cost effective, and you might be better off just buying a new machine.

Has this ever happened to you? You are in the middle of trying to finish up a project on your computer, when it suddenly freezes ominously, or worse, you see the "Blue Screen of Death" (**the blue screen with white text telling you that your computer has stopped working**).

What causes a computer to crash?
1. A computer crash can be caused by a number of things, including:
2. An outdated or misbehaving device driver,
3. A computer virus,
4. A corrupted program, or
5. A problem with your computer's memory.

What to Do When Your Computer Crashes:
1. The first thing to do is write down any error messages, exactly as they appear. This can be very helpful if you need to speak to a technical support person about the problem. Having at least a few clues to the cause of the problem will help them help you better and faster.
2. Next, restart your computer, and then open any documents you were working on to see what, if anything, was lost. If you were working in Microsoft Office Word, for example, you might see a pane with recent versions of the document that were saved before or during the crash.
3. If your computer won't start, or it starts but Windows won't start, you might have a more serious problem. Try starting your computer using Last Known Good Configuration. This is a Windows start-up option that uses the most recent system settings that worked correctly.
4. If using Last Known Good Configuration doesn't help, contact your computer manufacturer's technical support team. Even if your hard disk has failed, you can sometimes recover data from it. (See the previous section).

It's often possible to un-delete a file if you accidentally deleted something you need.

Here's How to Do It:
1. First, try to retrieve the file from the Recycle Bin.
If you accidentally deleted text from a Microsoft Word document and then saved (but didn't close) the document, you can sometimes get that text back:
1. First, try using the "Undo" function (click **File**, click **Edit**, and then click **Undo** in most versions of Word).
2. If you didn't save the document, closing it without saving it undoes all the changes you made since opening it.
3. If you've already closed the document, it might be too late to recover the deleted text.

NOTE: Files deleted from network shares don't go to the Recycle Bin, but your network administrator might be able to help you retrieve a file deleted from a network folder. If the file was deleted from a folder on your computer and you can't recover it from the Recycle Bin, try searching the Internet for "un-delete" to find freeware and shareware tools that can do the job.

Get the latest Updates to help prevent future crashes:
Windows XP users:
Go to Microsoft Update to find the latest drivers for your devices, or check the device manufacturer's website.

Windows Vista users:
1. Go to Windows Update for driver updates.
2. Open Windows Update by clicking the **Start** button , clicking **All Programs**, and then clicking **Windows Update**.
3. In the left pane, click **Check for updates**.
Windows 7 Users:
In Windows 7, Windows Update is now part of **Action Center,** which makes updating your PC even more convenient. To check for updates, just click the Action Center **icon** on the task bar.
Windows 8 Users:
1. Open the Control Panel (icons view), and click on the Windows Update icon.
2. In the left pane, click on the Change settings link.
3. Do step 4, 5, 6, or 7 below for what you would like to do.
4. To Turn On Automatic Updating
NOTE: This is the default setting. This setting will check for and have updates automatically downloaded in the background when your PC is not on a metered internet connection. Updates will be automatically in-stalled during the maintenance window with this setting.
A) In the drop down menu under important updates, select Install up-dates automatically.
B) Click on the maintenance window link to set the automatic maintenance window for what time you would like to have updates checked for and installed, and if you would like to wake up your computer to do so.
NOTE: By default, the time is set to 3:00 AM.
C) Go to step 8 below.
5. To Have Updates Downloaded Automatically but Let you Choose to Install them or Not
NOTE: Updates will be automatically downloaded in the background when your PC is not on a metered internet connection. Updates will not be automatically installed during the maintenance window with this setting.
A) In the drop down menu under important updates, select Check for updates but let me choose whether to install them.

B) Go to step 8 below.

6. **To Check for Updates Automatically but Let you Choose to Download and Install them or Not**

NOTE: Updates will not be automatically installed during the maintenance window with this setting.

A) In the drop down menu under Important updates, select Check for updates but let me choose whether to download and install them.

B) Go to step 8 below.

7. **To turn off Automatic Updating**

NOTE: Updates will not be automatically installed during the maintenance window with this setting.

A) In the drop down menu under important updates, select Never check for updates.

B) Go to step 8 below.

8. If you like, you can choose how you would like the other recommended updates and Microsoft Update settings to be set as.

9. When finished, click on OK.

10. If prompted by UAC, then click on Yes.

11. If you turned on automatic updating, then Windows will check for new updates now.

Blue Screen of Death

If you regularly get the "Blue Screen of Death," you may have a random access memory (RAM) problem.

A **"Blue Screen"** is the name given to the blue screen of strange numbers and information that can sometimes come up if your machine crashes. Essentially any *blue screen, hang, crash* or *lock-up* that happens after the Windows logo is displayed, falls into this category. Secondly, if that hap-pens repeatedly during boot, it could be anything from a bad device driver to malware or a virus.

Here's What to Do:
1. The best first step to take is to attempt to boot in what's called "Safe Mode". Safe mode disables a number of operating system components, possibly avoiding the component that might be causing the problem.
2. Once in safe mode you can try running the system file checker, your anti-virus software, anti-spyware software, and possibly get

Windows Updates.
Note: The Microsoft website knowledgebase has an article on "A description of the Safe Mode Boot options in Windows XP" that details how to start Safe Mode, and its options.
3. If Safe Mode itself won't work, the next step back is something called the Recover Console. You can install it on your machine before problems happen, as described in the Microsoft Knowledge base article "How to Install and Use the Recovery Console in Windows XP".
4. Note the message on the blue screen, especially the numbers. You can go to Microsoft's support site check it.

5. Also, put the text of the error message in a search engine and check it on the Internet. 6. Assuming you can diagnose it, a memory problem is easy to fix.

7. If you can't find the diagnosis information you need online, you can try swapping out memory sticks from another computer. (Note: That the memory must be of the same type).

8. If all else fails, take the old memory to a computer store. The people there may be willing to test it for you.

How to Locate and Remove Memory Sticks:
1. Memory sticks are located in slots on the motherboard, near the micro-processor. They're about four inches long.
2. Remove the old memory and match it at the store. Be sure you get the same type.
3. When you press the new memory into the slot, you will probably have to use a little force.
The clips on each end will snap into place when the memory is seated properly.

Adding More Memory (RAM)

How To Add More Memory to Your Computer
If it suddenly seems that your computer can't keep up and the drive light is flickering like crazy, it's probably time to install RAM. **Random Access Memory** or **(RAM)** is the primary working memory in a computer used for the temporary storage of programs and data and in which the data can be accessed directly and modified. It is the part of the computer that processes information. When a program is started, it is loaded into RAM to be run. RAM is like a workbench, and the larger this workbench is, the larger the files are that can be worked on it. So, the more RAM you have in your computer, the better it will work.

Important: Determine how much RAM you have and how much you need
Before you buy your new ram, you need to know how much memory you have and what type of memory to buy. You can do this by opening the **System Information** dialog box to see the installed physical memory on your computer, or you can go to Control Panel.
Note: The fast and easy way to figure out how to add RAM to your computer, is to use the memory advisory tool. It is a free downloadable tool that can scan your computer and figure out what memory you have, how much more memory will fit and then recommend the correct memory chip. It takes the guesswork out of upgrading memory.

First, Find out how much RAM your computer has installed Here's How to Do It:
1. Open System Information, click **Start**, click **All Programs**.
2. Next, click **Accessories**, click **System Tools**, and then click **System Information**.
3. In the left pane, select **System Summary**. The Installed Physical Memory (RAM) entry in the list tells you how much RAM your computer has.

Next, In Windows, go to the Start menu, click Settings, and then click Control Panel. Click System, and then select the General tab. At the bottom of the page you will see the amount of RAM.

Find out how much RAM you need.
The amount of RAM you need depends on the operating system you are using. For systems running **Windows8, 7, Windows Vista, or Windows XP,** you should have the minimum recommended amount, but more sometimes can be better, depending on your needs.

Note: If you just use your PC for browsing the Internet and writing letters, you may need only the minimum amount of RAM required to run the version of Windows you have installed on your computer. But for the best performance, especially if you keep several programs open at the same time while you're working; consider increasing the RAM on your computer to at least 2 gigabytes (GB).

Figure out what type of RAM you need
There are several ways to determine the maximum amount of RAM your computer can handle along with the speed:
1. Consult your PC owner's manual, which should show you the number of slots (**the place where you insert the RAM**), how much RAM each slot can take, and the maximum RAM your system can use.
2. Contact the manufacturer or use an online memory advisor tool. The online memory advisors use information that you enter about your computer model to do a memory check for your specific PC that tells you which products will work with your system.
3. To find out what kind of module you need, you can also open up your computer.

Adding More Memory (RAM) Con't.

Here's How to Do It:
1. First, shut off power to the computer, but leave it plugged in so that it's automatically grounded. **(Advanced Users).**
(Note: *If you have a computer that should not remain plugged in while work is being done on it, follow these steps:*
1.Turn off the computer and unplug the power cord.
2. Then, press the button that turns on the power to your computer.
This action helps you to be sure that there is no residual power to the memory slots or the computer's motherboard. The board also may have an LED light that is lit, which is another indication that there is residual power. Computers that should not remain plugged in will be clearly marked.)
3. Next, place the computer on a clean flat surface, and carefully remove the cover.
4. Ground Yourself by touching the metal case - *By touching the case, it discharges static electricity that could otherwise damage your computer's circuitry. Anti-static wrist straps are recommended, but this is not necessary for home users.*
5. Locate the RAM modules on the motherboard. They are green with black tubes.
6. Next determine the type of module you have. You can identify the type by its appearance.

Example:
1. DDR SDRAM is the most popular and looks like regular RAM but has one notch.
2. RDRAM is paired up (*you have to put in two at a time*) and has metal casing on one side.
3. SDRAM (which is being phased out) has two notches.

Adding More Memory (RAM) Con't.

---

4. Note your RAM speed, which is usually written on the side of the existing chip (either 266 or 333).
5. If you don't have a free slot, remove one of the memory cards to check the number of notches on it.
6. Replace the smaller of the two RAM modules.

Installing Your New RAM
Here's How to Do It:
1. Turn off the computer, and touch the metal casing.

Note: If you have a computer that should not remain plugged in while work is being done on it, turn off the computer and unplug the power cord. Then, press the button that turns on the power to your computer. This action helps you to be sure that there is no residual power to the memory slots or the computer's motherboard. The board also may have an LED light that is lit, which is another indication that there is residual power.

2. Open the compartment where your RAM is installed. You may have to remove screws to open the compartment. Note that this example is for a laptop computer. If you have a desktop computer, refer to the user manual to locate the RAM. You will have to remove the computer's cover.

Adding More Memory (RAM) Con't.

---

3. Locate the RAM modules (RAM cards). Find the empty slot where you plan to add a module, or remove the RAM module you are replacing.
4. Line up the notches of the new RAM module, and apply firm pressure to attach.
5. After you're sure the RAM module is snugly in place, close the latch at either end. If you have clips, they should snap back in place.
6. Reconnect all the cables, but leave the casing open until you're sure everything is working right.
7. Turn your computer back on. If you've installed everything correctly, the system will detect the new RAM.
Note: If the machine starts to beep, the memory is either incompatible or not correctly in its slot.
8. Check your system information to see how much RAM you now have.

Example: If you replaced a 512-MB module with a 1-GB one, you should have 1 GB (1,024 MB) minus 512 , or 512 MB more RAM than you did previously. If you added the RAM but didn't remove any, you should have 1 GB more RAM, for a total of 1.5 GB.

9. Try one of your programs that wasn't working well. If it still isn't working, unplug everything again and get back into the computer to check that the RAM modules are firmly secured. Once the RAM is installed, your Windows 95/98/ME/2000/NT/XP/Vista /Windows 7/8 system will automatically detect the new memory and start using it. Apple computers will do this as well.

IP Address

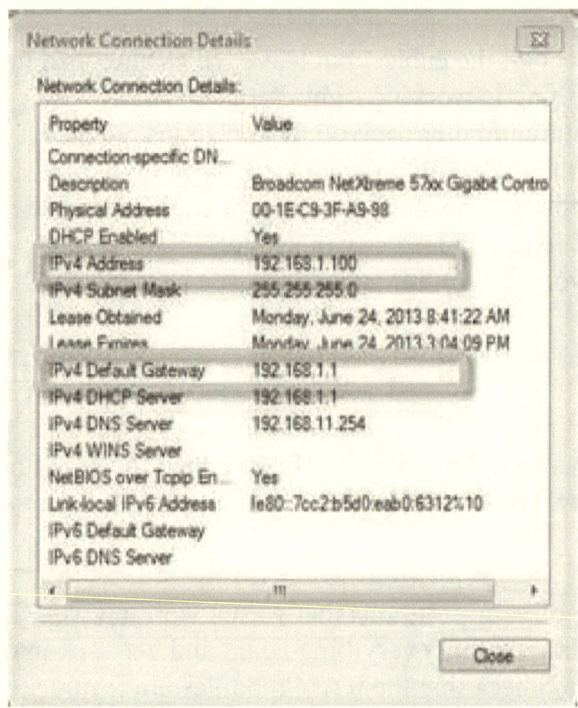

How can I change my IP address?

If you're concerned about privacy, or wish to throw off marketers that track your surfing habits, the following steps will show you how to easily change your IP address in **Windows 7, 8,** and **Vista** and **XP.**

First, the simplest thing to do to change your IP address is to try turning off (or unplugging) the power of your Cable/DSL modem for *five minutes*. In many cases this will change your IP address. However, if that does not change your IP address, repeat the process for 8 hours (*overnight works even better*) instead of five minutes. Doing this should result in an IP change.
If the above methods do not result in your IP address changing, you can choose the option below that best matches your configuration, and try the steps listed to change your IP address that way.

Note: Unfortunately in some cases (*when you have a dynamically assigned IP address*), you will not be able to change your IP address using these methods, as it is ultimately determined by your ISP's DHCP configuration.

Important Note: It is very important that you follow those steps very closely. In particular, the instructions for **disconnecting** and **reconnecting** hardware, and turning hardware ON/OFF, are extremely important.

Windows - First Option
Computer connected directly to the modem:
1. Get to a command prompt. (by clicking START, run, cmd).
2. Type "ipconfig /release" (without the quotes, on the command line by itself).
3. Type "ipconfig /renew" (without the quotes, on the command line by itself).

How to Change IP Address Con't.

Windows - Second Option
Computer connected directly to the modem
1. Get to a command prompt. (by clicking START, run, cmd).
2. Type "ipconfig /release" (without the quotes).
3. Shut down computer.
4. Turn off all ethernet hubs/switches.
5. Turn off cable/DSL modem.
6. Leave off overnight.
7. Then turn everything back on.

Third Option - Network with Router
1. Log into the router's admin console. (Example http://192.168.1.1/)
2. Release the IP address. (Method varies by router manufacturer)
3. Turn off router, ethernet hubs/switches, and the cable/DSL modem.
4. Leave off overnight.
5. Then turn everything back on.
If you are using a cable/DSL modem and a router, you can connect your computer directly to the cable/DSL modem. This allows your ISP's DHCP to issue you a new (hopefully changed) IP address based of the (hardware) MAC address of your computer's ethernet card.

Please note: This could significantly impact your system's security.
1. If all the above methods has not worked to change your IP address and you have a router, check and see if there is a *"Clone MAC Address"* option.

How to Change IP Address Con't.

Using it should change your IP address; however, in most cases you'll only be able to do it once.

2. If all else fails contact your internet service provider (ISP) and ask them if they are able to change your IP address or how long your connection needs to be off for your IP address to change.

3. You can attempt to configure your internet browser to use a proxy server if you are trying to change your IP address in order to access web based forums, or other sites.

Whatever the case may be, be sure to also delete your browser cookies after making the changes above. Cookies can also be used to track your browsing habits, and failure to clear them may render your IP change useless.

COMPUTER PROCESSOR (CPU)

Upgrading the Processor (CPU)

Despite the high clock speeds and high heat dissipation of modern CPUs, it's a fairly rare occurrence when a CPU actually fails. The CPU upgrade is perhaps one of the simpler upgrades to perform on your computer. If you've done it before, replacing a CPU isn't particularly challenging, but it can be a little intimidating for a first timer.

Steps Involved:
Upgrading the CPU involves:
1. Determining the effectiveness of the upgrade
2. Selecting the right CPU for your system.
3. Uninstalling the existing CPU and
4. Installing the new CPU

First, determine if a CPU upgrade is necessary.
1. If your computer is at most a few years old and all you do is browse the web, check email, and write papers, then you probably do not need a new CPU.

2. If you play the latest games, edit photos, or encode video, then a CPU upgrade may be appropriate.

If your computer has become sluggish and now you are thinking about a CPU upgrade, first check to see if the CPU is the cause of the slowdown. To do that, check to see if the programs you run are CPU intensive.
1. Use the Task Manager to monitor your CPU usage
2. To access the Task Manager, click Ctrl-Alt-Del at the same time.
3. Next select the Performance tab.
4. Then, continue using your computer regularly. When you are done check the "CPU Usage History" graph in the 'Task Manager' to see if your computing tasks are CPU intensive.
You will know that they are if the majority of the graph is at or near 100%. If your computing tasks are CPU intensive, then a CPU upgrade will most likely improve the performance of your computer.

Next determine whether it is practical and possible to upgrade your CPU.

1. Use diagnostic software or check the manual to determine what type of CPU you have.

Note: Once you have determined the type of CPU in your machine, you need to find out what options are available for your system. If for example, your particular computer already has a top-of-the-line CPU, then your options may be limited and any possible upgrade would bring very little benefit.

If you have determined that upgrading your CPU is in-deed viable and possible, it is time to acquire the new CPU.

Here's How to Perform the Upgrade:

First, remove your existing CPU by following these steps:

1. Unplug your computer, open the case, and ground yourself to prevent static damage.

2. The first step to replace a CPU is to remove the heat sink. Note: All modern CPU's require an active heat sink, (*a chunk of finned heat-conductive metal with a cooling fan mounted on top*). The only rule of thumb for removing heat sinks is to study the latching mechanism then use your thumb to release it.

3. Remove the HSF unit. You may need to use a flathead screwdriver to push down the clip holding the HSF to the socket. Be very careful with this step.

4. Unplug the CPU fan from its power source (either the motherboard or a Molex connector).

5. Remove the old CPU by pulling out and up the plastic or metal lever, and then lifting out the CPU by its sides.

Note: All modern CPUs since the inception of Socket 7 have used ZIF (Zero Insertion Force) sockets, where the CPU legs are locked in place by moving a locking lever.

Reverse the above steps to install the new CPU: 1. Insert the new CPU, being sure to match the pins to the holes. The CPU will *only* fit in one direction and *will not* require any force to insert. If you need to force it in, the CPU is incorrectly oriented. Once the CPU is in the socket, lower and lock the lever.

Upgrading the Processor (CPU) Con't.

2. Apply a thin layer of thermal compound to the CPU core, if your HSF unit does not have some already.
3. Next, install the HSF unit, being sure to orient the HSF unit such that the CPU core is completely flush against the bottom of the heat sink.
Note: Again, you may need a flathead screwdriver. You must also be very careful with this step so as not to damage the CPU and/or the mother-board. Remember, if you power up your system without the HSF unit properly attached, you will cause permanent damage to the CPU!
4. Plug the CPU fan into the proper power source.
5. Before closing the case and finalizing the installation, plug in the power cord, and turn on your computer to verify that the new CPU is working properly.
Confirm that the CPU fan is spinning.

Carefully touch the heat sink to make sure it is warm.

Check the CPU temperature in the BIOS to make sure the temperature is not rising rapidly.

Verify that you can boot into your operating system.

If all of the above checks out, you have successfully upgraded your CPU. You can now shut down the computer, and close the case.

Important: Know your limitations
Some things may be beyond your ability to do. For instance, upgrading a microprocessor can be dicey. Even if a faster microprocessor will fit in your motherboard, you probably need to upgrade the BIOS (Basic Input Output System). This is done through a process called *"flashing"*, in which information is downloaded to change the BIOS. **Note:** If flashing isn't done correctly, the computer can be rendered useless. It is advised to leave this to the experts.

Windows 8 Tips, Tricks, and Shortcuts.

INTRODUCTION

Windows 8 has been out for quite some time now, and if you are used to previous versions of Windows O.S; then you're going to notice the drastically different user interface this new version of Windows ushered in. In fact, Windows 8 has seen the biggest change since the jump from Windows 3.1 to Windows 95. Even experienced PC users may be left feeling a little lost... Just figuring out something as simple as shutting down your PC can be challenging with Windows 8.

In part, that's because Windows 8 is **two** Operating Systems in one. There's the traditional Windows desktop, which is basically Windows 7 (*it runs the 4 million existing Windows programs*), then there's a new environment designed for tablets and laptops that sport touch-enabled displays. Out goes the Start menu, in comes the new touch-oriented Start screen with new Windows 8-style apps and new interface conventions.

Most new PCs will come with Windows 8, and if Microsoft is correct about the world moving to touch screen PCs, sooner or later you'll find a Windows 8 machine under your fingertips. Don't despair though, help is at hand. I have researched every part of Windows 8, uncovering many of its most important tips, tricks and shortcuts and have listed them in this guide so you can navigate, be more productive and learn your way around Windows 8 as quickly as possible. You will soon be equipped to get the most out of Microsoft's latest release, have some fun and make the new Windows 8 OS a worthwhile choice. With these tips, tricks and shortcuts you won't need to spend hours or weeks poking around online for help!

1. Log in without a username or password:

To speed up the Windows 8 log-in process, you may want to disable the **username** and **password** log-in screen. You can do so by opening the Run window (**press the Windows key + R**) and typing in **"netplwiz"** to access the User Accounts dialog box. Uncheck the box near the top that says **"Users must enter a user name and password to use this computer."** Click *OK,* and enter the **username** and **password** one last **time to confirm your choice, and you are all set for easy access to your system.**

2. Windows 8 scanner problems:

Some people are finding it difficult to get Windows 8 drivers for all the devices. Consequently, when there is a lack of adequate Windows 8 drivers, the respective devices won't work properly. Same is the case with the scanner too. The only way around this is to run the existing drivers in compatibility mode.

Follow these Instructions to resolve these Windows 8 problems with the scanner device by running the existing device driver in compatibility mode.

1. Click on the ".EXE" file for your scanners driver.
2. Click on "Compatibility tab"> "Run this program in compatibility mode" > "Run this program as an ad-ministrator" > "Apply" > "Ok".
3. Finally finish the procedure to fix your Windows 8 scanner problems by double clicking on the "EXE" file.

3. Using Windows 8 apps and your desktop simultaneously:

Because the Windows 8 experience is split between new Windows 8 Store apps and old-school desktop apps, the operating system is prone to some strange behaviors. Case in point: When running a multi-monitor setup, Windows 8 apps will consume your main screen, leaving your secondary screen running the desktop. This arrangement would seem to allow full-screen multitasking among both types of apps—a modern app on the left side, a desktop app on the right side—but this isn't the case.

Indeed, as soon as you begin using the desktop on your secondary screen, the new-style Windows 8 app disappears, and your primary screen begins running the desktop.

Here is how to work around this problem: On your primary screen, use the new Windows 8 split-screen **"snapping"** function to run the desktop and a new Windows 8 Store app together. The desktop can take up the left-hand sliver, while the Windows 8 app consumes the majority of the screen. Now use your **second** display for a full desktop view. In this arrangement, you can fully multitask between new-style apps and desktop apps, and both windows will be large enough to be useful.

4. **Adjust 'SmartScreen' settings:**
By default, you need an administrator's permission, but this can easily be adjusted to just a warning or no indication at all. Using the magic search function described above, type **"security"** at the Start screen and find the **"Check security status"** in the Settings tab. From this area, you can adjust various security settings, including the Windows SmartScreen.

5. **Turn Live Tiles on and off:**
When looking at the plethora of tiles on your Start screen, the view can get stagnant, despite all the pretty colors. This is where Live Tiles come in. They offer real-time data right on your Start screen, and you don't need to open any apps. For example, the Weather tile will show you the current conditions, and Mail will show you the subject of the latest message you've received.
You can customize which apps are live and which aren't by right-clicking on the tiles. A settings bar on the bottom will pop up with an option to turn the Live Tile on or off. Simply select the preferred option, and you're all set. Note, however, that not all apps have a live, real-time data-streaming option.

6. Use centralized, contextual Search Function:

The Search function located on the Charms bar is packed with power, letting you search the directories of not only your Windows 8 machine, but also the greater Windows cyber-system. Simply choose the collection of data you want to sift through—it could be all your installed apps, your system settings, your files, your mail messages, or even an external service like the Windows Store or Bing Maps—type in a keyword, and hit Enter. The Search function will then return the results, perfectly contextualized for the database you've addressed

By the way, you don't even need to hit the Charms bar to access Search. From the Start screen, simply start typing, and you'll be quickly taken to the text-entry field for search queries.

7. Start Screen Zoom Feature:

The Start Screen is full of nice, big, chunky tiles that represent all your apps. The tiles are easy to see in small groups, but what if you have hundreds of apps installed? Most will be hidden from view, unless you want to do a lot of scrolling. Enter the new semantic zoom feature. If you're using a touch display, squeeze the Start screen with two fingers to receive a bird's eye view of your entire screen contents. And the feature is also available to mouse and keyboard users: Simply hold down the Ctrl button, and use your mouse wheel to zoom in and out.

8. Using the Quick Access Menu:

With Windows 8 some has found it very confusing to open apps as well as search for items, as compared to the standard desktop user interface found in previous Windows OS's. Besides, the Hot Corner feature was also not to everyone's taste. However, you can easily bypass this feature during startup by downloading and installing the Windows 8 Start Menu Toggle.

Using this, you can skip the complex start menu of the Metro UI. Bring up the Quick Access Menu by right-clicking on the lower left of the screen—whether you're in the Windows 8 Start screen or in the desktop—will enable a direct line to many key system management chores, including Disk Management, Task Manager, Device Manager, and Control Panel.

9. Closing an application:

In Windows 8 a problem that has raised concern is the way apps close after use **(you will quickly notice that close buttons are hard to find).** Once you have used an app and exited from it, the app is not closed. **That's because Microsoft encourages us to run apps in the background where they'll take up minimal resources, but still be accessible at any time.** The CPU only closes the app when it wants to save CPU cycles. Hence Metro apps always remain in the background, which is more like the functioning of **smartphone apps**. However, this is not desired by many users as they would prefer the apps to be closed after use, because a lot of system memory could get used up if the apps run in the background, that could create performance issues as well. Moreover, apps could be stuck while in use which may prove to be very irritating for people especially when they are using it on an emergency basis.

The best solution for this problem is to open the Task Manager and kill all the processes manually.
Or, if you prefer, you can close an app by dragging it with your mouse or finger from the top of the screen all the way down to the bottom. As you drag, the app will minimize into a thumbnail, and when you reach the bottom, it will disappear from view. Alternatively, you can still close apps via Alt + F4 and through the Task Manager.

10. Categorize Your Start Screen Apps:

Your Start screen can become a cluttered mess if you collect too many apps and other elements that have been pinned to the screen as tiles. In Windows 8 you can take advantage of built-in organization tools that let you divide everything into labeled groups.

First, drag all the tiles you want to assign to a single group to the far right-hand side of your Start screen in vacant territory; the OS should sequester the tiles together. Once you're satisfied with your assembly, use semantic zoom (described above) to get a bird's eye view of your desktop. Now right-click the group (or simply drag down on it), and select the "Name group" option on the left of the bar that appears below. Type in the name, and enjoy your newly organized Start screen!

11. How to Create a Picture Password:

Using a picture password is a fun way to keep your computer secure while not having to remember a complex password. To enable this, press the **Windows key + I** to get to the settings charm. Click **"Change PC settings"** at the bottom right, and go to the Users tab. Under **"Sign-in options"** will be the **"Create a picture password"** button. This will give you the option to choose any picture, and then define three gestures anywhere on the image. Your gestures can be circles, swipes and clicks.
For example, to set a picture password for the image above, you could click on the highest palm tree; draw a circle around the island, and then swipe down from the lens flare in the upper right. Just beware: **(The direction of each gesture matters).** After confirming it a couple times, your picture password will be set.

12. Using the Start-8 Utility:

One of biggest complaints about Windows 8 is that it boots straight to the Start screen—an annoyance for many committed desktop users. The **Start8 utility** helps you avoid this situation, and you can actually boot straight to the desktop without installing anything extra.

Go to the start screen and type in **"schedule"** to search for Schedule Task in Settings. Click on **Task Scheduler Library** to the left, and select **Create Task.** Name your task something like **"Boot to desktop."** Now select the **Triggers** tab, choose **New,** and use the drop-down box to select starting the task **"At log on."** Click *OK* and go to the **Actions** tab, choose **New,** and enter **"explorer"** for the Program/Script value.

Press *OK*, save the task, and restart the computer to test it out!

13. Locate the Windows games folder:

Currently, the games folder used in Windows 7 aren't present in Windows 8. But don't worry; if you install any current-generation PC game that would regularly save to this folder, the folder is automatically created. For a quick way to find it, right-click on the game icon on the Start screen and choose **"Open file location"** at the bottom.

14. Adjust your privacy settings:

A lot of apps tap into very personal information by default. Indeed, your pictures, location, and name are liberally woven throughout the system, and like many users you may not be comfortable trusting your machine with that much sensitive data. To adjust the settings, press the Windows key + I, and go to Change PC Settings. Select the Privacy option, and personalize the settings for your personal data there.

15. Task Manager for Startup items:

You no longer have to run the **MSConfig** program to change startup items. Startup items now show up in a tab on Task Manager. Simply press Ctrl + Alt + Del and select Task Manager. Click the **"More details"** tab at the bottom and find the Startup tab at the top.

16. Start Windows 8 in Safe Mode:

Safe Mode is a great way to get into your system when something won't allow you to start up normally. Troubleshooting becomes a breeze when corrupted drivers and files aren't loaded that prevents a system from functioning. It used to be as easy as pressing F8 when the system starts up, but doing so with Windows 8 will take you to Automatic Repair Mode. The trick to getting back to good old fashioned Safe Mode? Hold down the Shift key and press F8 while booting up.

This takes you to the Recovery mode. Select **"advanced options,"** then **"troubleshoot,"** then the **"advanced options"** again. Select **Windows Startup Settings** and finally the **Restart** button. This will reboot the computer and give you the option to boot into Safe Mode.
If you need to get into Safe Mode from within Windows, open the dialog box (the Windows key + R) and type "**msconfig**" (no quote marks). Select the *Boot* tab and check the **Safe boot** box. The system will continually boot into Safe Mode until you go back and uncheck the box.

17. Pin a Shutdown Button Onto the Bottom of Your Desktop:

Windows 8 hides the Power button in the Settings menu, forcing a multistep process just to shut down one's PC. But thanks to a crafty shortcut trick, you can pin a Shutdown button right onto the bottom of your desktop.

Here's how:

To create a shortcut on your desktop, (right-click, and go to **New, then Shortcut).** Enter **"shutdown /s /t 0"** (with no quotes, and, yes, that's a zero not an "O") as the location of the item, and press *Next*. Now name the shortcut (preferably **"Shutdown")** and press **Finish.**

Right-click the shortcut, and navigate to **Properties.** Choose **Change Icon in** the Shortcut tab, and then *OK* to leave the warning box. Choose an icon of your choice from the list. In the screenshot above, you'll see we chose a Power button.

Right-click the shortcut again, and select **Pin to Start.** You can place the icon on your Start screen wherever it's convenient. Clicking it will instantly shut down your computer.

18. Windows 8 Share Feature:

Windows 8 is Microsoft's first social-media-aware PC operating system. Using the Share button located on the Charms bar, you can pick any number of elements from your Windows 8 Store apps—say, a location from your Maps app, a news story from the Finance app, or a even a contact from your People app—and then distribute that item to friends via other Windows 8 programs. Perhaps most conveniently, you can quickly share a photo via email or Twitter, or to your own SkyDrive or Windows Phone. The Share button is contextual, and the more you use it, the more you'll discover which apps share with each other, and which don't. (

NOTE: None of your desktop apps offer sharing opportunities through the Charms menu.

19. Time For a Refresh:

If your system is feeling a little sluggish, it may be time for a refresh. In the past we would have to find our copy of Windows 7, back up all of our data, and perform a fresh install to enjoy that back-to-factory-fresh feeling. But now Windows 8 allows you to perform a fresh install from within Windows without losing any data.

In order to perform the refresh, go to Settings and click the **Change PC Settings** tab near the bottom. Select the **General** tab and find the "Refresh your PC without affecting your files" section near the middle (you may also select "Remove everything and reinstall Windows" to get the true factory settings treatment). Select "Get started" and press "Refresh." After a few minutes the PC will restart, and you will have a fresh copy of Windows 8.

20. Activate Family Safety Feature:

Want to avoid some unwanted surprises on your credit card? Create a separate, standard account on the device for your kids (NOTE: Family Safety can't be applied to an administrator account). You can activate Family Safety by going to the **Control Panel, User Accounts,** and **Family Safety,** and selecting the account you would like to apply it to. From these settings you can get reports on the account's activity; set a level of Web filtering; set time limits; and enforce Windows Store, game, and app restrictions.

21. Windows 8 Has No 'Delete Confirmation Message':

In Windows 8 the 'Delete Confirmation Message' has been removed. Un-like in the previous OS versions, whenever you delete an item from your PC, you get a confirmation prompt to decide whether or not to really de-lete the app.
This feature is absent in Windows 8 as once you select the delete option, the item is moved to the Recycle Bin without any prompt. But luckily, you can restore it from the recycle bin if you accidentally deleted it.

22. Installing Windows Media Center In Win-dows 8 Pro

Windows Media Center is a program developed by Microsoft, which al-lows users to manage as well as play music & videos. It also offers an op-tion to stream and record live videos.

There are many third party websites, which offer downloading Windows 8 and Windows Media Center free. You can try Windows Media Center with Windows 8 Pro by opting any of the options. Just sign up for the Windows Media Center and you will re-ceive a license key through mail.

Follow the guidelines below to install the utility in your system run-ning on Windows 8 Pro.
1. Before you start the installation procedure, go to your email inbox, and copy the license key to your computer.
2. On the desktop of your computer, access the Charms bar, either drag-ging your mouse pointer to the upper right corner of the screen, or by using the Win + C hotkey. Search "Add features."
3. Highlight "Settings" in the search results, and select "Add features to Windows 8."
4. Enter the product key as received in the mail and wait until the verifica-tion process completes. Windows will automatically download and install the Media Center to your computer.
5. Restart your computer when the installation is complete. Run Media Center either from the Start screen, or by searching for it.
6. When you launch Media Center for the first time, it will instruct you to set up the program. Click "Continue" on the window, and opt for either an Express setup (to go with the default settings), or custom setup.
7. After the setup is complete, you can start with organizing your media libraries with the Media Center.
Microsoft skipped providing support for this utility in the starter pack of Windows 8, but the program functions without any issues in Windows 8 Pro. While it is always better to opt for genuine Windows platform, downloading Windows 8 Pro from any third party websites also will not hinder installing the add-on to your computer.
Install the utility on your Windows 8 Pro computer and enjoy the features of the best media management suite for Microsoft Windows.

23. Windows 8 installation problems

Windows 8 can be installed on a computer, with a disc either downloaded from the Microsoft site, or purchased as a DVD. You can also create a USB drive version of the Windows 8 disc. The USB drive and the DVD Versions are often used to install the OS on laptops and desktops.

Windows 8 Problems During Installation - Blank /Black Screen Post-Installation:
A black/blank screen after installation of Windows 8 is a major problem faced by a lot of users. They usually have no idea as to what could be the reason for this. During the installation process there are usually no prob-lems, but the problem of the blank screen arises only after the installation is complete. This Windows 8 problem could be fixed with help from Mi-crosoft Windows 8 support team. Alternatively, you can follow the below steps to do it yourself:
1. You can create a bootable Windows 8 Installation USB drive or DVD disk, and then do the install.
2. Check the BIOS settings for your computer, and enable the Plug And Play OS option.
3. Next, set the security software like the Antivirus and/or Firewall as dis-abled.
4. Download a fresh copy of Windows 8.

NOTE: When you are doing an upgrade of Windows 8, do a clean install if you face problems.
Missing Important Files /Drivers
The error message "Unable to install Windows 8 to this partition because of missing drivers, try to enter BIOS" during or after installing Windows 8, can be dealt with. To fix this problem, hold down the Alt key till your computer beeps during the reboot. Hold the Alt key down till the whirling gear shows on the screen, and then select your OS as startup drive. This type of problem solving is best suited for Macbook Air.

Post installation problems in Windows 8
Failed Upgrade
This problem is where the Windows 8 upgrade fails .It could have many reasons. Firstly, make sure that your system meets the minimum require-ments for a Windows 8 installation. Next, disable the security programs to allow for a smooth upgrade. Then, there should be a fast and uninterrupt-ed internet connection. The Windows 8 copy should be valid and li-censed. Where the touch- based functionality is made use of, see that your computer supports multi-touch function.
Even after all this, if you face problems, you can contact the Windows support teams. The Windows 8 problems can be resolved by availing help from them.

List of Windows 8 hotkey commands:
Press the Windows key to enter the tiled Start screen.

The Windows key + M minimizes everything that's showing on the desktop.

The Windows key + E opens Explorer for quick access to folders.

On the Start screen, press the Windows key + D to instantly get to the desktop.

The Windows key + Tab opens a list of currently running programs.

The Windows key + Print Screen takes a screenshot and saves it in a Screenshots folder nested in your Pictures folder.

To take a screenshot on a Windows 8 tablet, simultaneously press the Windows button and the volume-down button on the tablet chassis.

The Windows key + Q opens a global search menu. Type what you're looking for and where you would like to look.

The Windows key + W opens a search in your system settings to quickly locate and change system properties.

The Windows key + F opens a file and folder search.

The Windows key + Pause opens the system properties page to show you a quick rundown of your specs.

The Windows key + "," (that's the comma sign!) makes all current windows transparent, giving you a peek at the desktop as long as you hold down the Windows key.

The Windows key + "." (The period) snaps a window to the right or left side (toggling each time you press ".").

The Windows key + R prompts the Run command—useful for quickly launching apps and other routines with a command prompt.

The Windows key + X opens the Quick Access Menu, exposing system functionality such as the Command Prompt, Disk Management, File Explorer, Run, and more. Alternatively, you can right-click on the bottom right corner of the screen to spawn the Quick Access Menu.

The Windows key + I opens the settings menu, giving you quick access to the Control Panel, Personalization, and your Power button, among other features.

The Windows key + O locks orientation on devices with an accelerometer.

Basic DOS Commands

Command	Description	Type
ansi.sys	Defines functions that change display graphics, control cursor movement, and reassign keys.	File
append	Causes MS-DOS to look in other direc-tories when editing a file or running a command.	External
arp	Displays, adds, and removes arp infor-mation from network devices.	External
assign	Assign a drive letter to an alternate let-ter.	External
assoc	View the file associations.	Internal
at	Schedule a time to execute commands or programs.	External
atmadm	Lists connections and addresses seen by Windows ATM call manager.	Internal
attrib	Display and change file attributes.	External
batch	Recovery console	Recovery

	command that exe-cutes a series of commands in a file.	
bootcfg	Recovery console command that allows a user to view, modify, and rebuild the boot.ini	Recovery
break	Enable / disable CTRL + C feature.	Internal
cacls	View and modify file ACL's.	External
call	Calls a batch file from another batch file.	Internal
cd	Changes directories.	Internal
chcp	Supplement the International keyboard and character set information.	External
chdir	Changes directories.	Internal
chdsk	Check the hard disk drive running FAT for errors.	External
chkntfs	Check the hard disk drive running NTFS for errors.	External
choice	Specify a listing of multiple options within a batch file.	External
cls	Clears the screen.	Internal
cmd	Opens the command interpreter.	
color	Easily change the foreground and background color of the MS-DOS window.	Internal

command	Opens the command interpreter.	
comp	Compares files.	External
compact	Compresses and uncompress files.	External
control	Open Control Panel icons from the MS-DOS prompt.	External
convert	Convert FAT to NTFS.	External
copy	Copy files to an alternate location.	Internal
ctty	Change the computers input/output devices.	Internal
date	View or change the systems date.	Internal
debug	Debug utility to create assembly programs to modify hardware settings.	External
defrag	Re-arrange the hard disk drive to help with loading programs.	External
del	Deletes one or more files.	Internal
delete	Recovery console command that deletes a file.	Internal
deltree	Deletes one or more files or directories.	External
dir	List the contents of one or more directory.	Internal
disable	Recovery console command that disables Windows system services or drivers.	Recovery
diskcomp	Compare a disk with another disk.	External
diskcopy	Copy the contents of one disk and place them on another disk.	External
doskey	Command to view and execute commands that have been run in the past.	External
dosshell	A GUI to help with early MS-DOS	External

users.

drivparm	Enables overwrite of original device drivers.	Internal
echo	Displays messages and enables and disables echo.	Internal
edit	View and edit files.	External
edlin	View and edit files.	External
emm386	Load extended Memory Manager.	External
ename	Recovery console command to enable a disable service or driver.	Recovery
endlocal	Stops the localization of the environment changes enabled by the setlocal command.	Internal
erase	Erase files from computer.	Internal
exit	Exit from the command interpreter.	Internal
expand	Expand a Microsoft Windows file back to it's original format.	External
extract	Extract files from the Microsoft Windows cabinets.	External
fasthelp	Displays a listing of MS-DOS commands and information about them.	External
fc	Compare files.	External
fdisk	Utility used to create partitions on the hard disk drive.	External
find	Search for text within a file.	External
findstr	Searches for a string of text within a file.	External
fixboot	Writes a new boot sector.	Recovery
fixmbr	Writes a new boot record to a disk drive.	Recovery

for	Boolean used in batch files.	Internal
format	Command to erase and prepare a disk drive.	External
ftp	Command to connect and operate on a FTP server.	External
ftype	Displays or modifies file types used in file extension associations.	Recovery
goto	Moves a batch file to a specific label or location.	Internal
graftabl	Show extended characters in graphics mode.	External
help	Display a listing of commands and brief explanation.	External
if	Allows for batch files to perform conditional processing.	Internal
ifshlp.sys	32-bit file manager.	External
ipconfig	Network command to view network adapter settings and assigned values.	External
keyb	Change layout of keyboard.	External
label	Change the label of a disk drive.	External
lh	Load a device driver in to high memory.	Internal
listsvc	Recovery console command that displays the services and drivers.	Recovery
loadfix	Load a program above the first 64k.	External
loadhigh	Load a device driver in to high memory.	Internal
lock	Lock the hard disk drive.	Internal
logoff	Logoff the currently profile using the computer.	External
logon	Recovery console command to list installations and enable administrator	Recovery

login.

map	Displays the device name of a drive.	Recovery
md	Command to create a new directory.	Internal
mem	Display memory on system.	External
mkdir	Command to create a new directory.	Internal
mode	Modify the port or display settings.	External
more	Display one page at a time.	External
move	Move one or more files from one directory to another directory.	Internal
msav	Early Microsoft Virus scanner.	External
msd	Diagnostics utility.	External
msdex	Utility used to load and provide access to the CD-ROM.	External
nbtstat	Displays protocol statistics and current TCP/IP connections using NBT	External
net	Update, fix, or view the network or network settings	External
netsh	Configure dynamic and static network information from MS-DOS.	External
netstat	Display the TCP/IP network protocol statistics and information.	External
nlsfunc	Load country specific information.	External
nslookup	Look up an IP address of a domain or host on a network.	External
path	View and modify the computers path location.	Internal
pathping	View and locate locations of network latency.	External
pause	Command used in batch files to stop the processing of a command.	Internal

ping	Test / send information to another network computer or network device.	External
popd	Changes to the directory or network path stored by the pushd command.	Internal
power	Conserve power with computer portables.	External
print	Prints data to a printer port.	External
prompt	View and change the MS-DOS prompt.	Internal
pushd	Stores a directory or network path in memory so it can be returned to at any time.	Internal
qbasic	Open the QBasic.	External
rd	Removes an empty directory.	Internal
ren	Renames a file or directory.	Internal
rename	Renames a file or directory.	Internal
rmdir	Removes an empty directory.	Internal
robocopy	A robust file copy command for the Windows command line.	
route	View and configure windows network route tables.	External
runas	Enables a user to run a program as a different user.	External
scandisk	Run the scandisk utility.	External
scanreg	Scan registry and recover registry from errors.	External
set	Change one variable or string to another.	Internal
setlocal	Enables local environments to be changed without affecting anything else.	Internal
setver	Change MS-DOS version to trick	External

older MS-DOS programs.

share	Installs support for file sharing and locking capabilities.	External
shift	Changes the position of replaceable parameters in a batch program.	Internal
shutdown	Shutdown the computer from the MS-DOS prompt.	External
smartdrv	Create a disk cache in conventional memory or extended memory.	External
sort	Sorts the input and displays the output to the screen.	External
start	Start a separate window in Windows from the MS-DOS prompt.	Internal
subst	Substitute a folder on your computer for another drive letter.	External
switches	Remove add functions from MS-DOS.	Internal
sys	Transfer system files to disk drive.	External
telnet	Telnet to another computer / device from the prompt.	External
time	View or modify the system time.	Internal
title	Change the title of their MS-DOS window.	Internal
tracert	Visually view a network packets route across a network.	External
tree	View a visual tree of the hard disk drive.	External
type	Display the contents of a file.	Internal
undelete	Undelete a file that has been deleted.	External
unformat	Unformat a hard disk drive.	External
unlock	Unlock a disk drive.	Internal

ver	Display the version information.	Internal
verify	Enables or disables the feature to determine if files have been written properly.	Internal
vol	Displays the volume information about the designated drive.	Internal
xcopy	Copy multiple files, directories, or drives from one location to another.	Internal